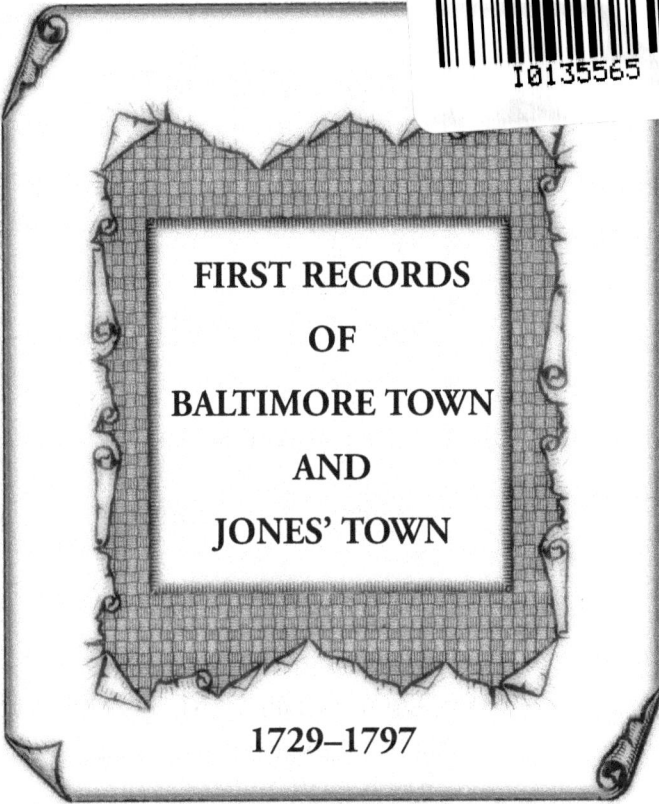

FIRST RECORDS

OF

BALTIMORE TOWN

AND

JONES' TOWN

1729–1797

M A R Y L A N D

City Council of Baltimore

HERITAGE BOOKS
2016

HERITAGE BOOKS

AN IMPRINT OF HERITAGE BOOKS, INC.

Books, CDs, and more—Worldwide

For our listing of thousands of titles see our website
at
www.HeritageBooks.com

A Facsimile Reprint
Published 2016 by
HERITAGE BOOKS, INC.
Publishing Division
5810 Ruatan Street
Berwyn Heights, Md. 20740

— Publisher's Notice —
In reprints such as this, it is often not possible to remove blemishes from
the original. We feel the contents of this book warrant its reissue despite
these blemishes and hope you will agree and read it with pleasure.

International Standard Book Numbers
Paperbound: 978-0-7884-1339-1
Clothbound: 978-0-7884-5970-2

The Enteries of Baltemore Town begun by George Walker December 1st 1729

Recivd february the 8th yAA in Ordsrl horrison Breenwood

TITLE PAGE OF THE FIRST BOOK OF BALTIMORE TOWN.
(*From photograph.*)

Preface

It may not be amiss to state that the records herein contained were printed in the main from the First Book of Baltimore Town. Viewed through modern spectacles the handiwork of the recordmaker of 1729 is a queer production.

In giving that handiwork to the general public—now upward of two hundred years after it was begun—an effort has been made to preserve the eccentricities of the English of the day, or, perhaps, as better expressed, the liberties taken with the English of the day have not been disturbed by the transplanting process. They are given very accurately in this—their typographical counterpart.

The pen has been faithfully followed by the type. The one object was to produce the records—spelling, punctuation and all, and to portray, as far as possible, general characteristics. To an extent, at least, this has been accomplished.

Nothing has been taken from; nothing added to the old book. It stands for itself. But its spelling—at times unique; its erratic punctuation (or lack of punctuation, as the matter may be); its quaint phraseology, though transferred from fading lines to printed pages, tell a story of early Baltimore that can be nothing but historically correct. Events were written at a time when history was being made; when the foundation of the now great City of Baltimore was laid.

The records begin with the first session of a Commission which was authorized to select a site for Baltimore Town. It is the doings of this Commission, or rather the Commissioners of Baltimore Town, relative the establishment of boundaries, laying out of streets, "taking up" of lots, etc., from 1729 to the incorporation of the City—1797, that are chronicled.

The printing of these archives will, if it accomplishes no other good, prevent wear and tear upon the originals, for it has not been possible to refuse all requests by those who desired to use the old books and manuscripts in search of information concerning early Baltimore. Likewise the perpetuation of the records is assured even though the originals should, by any lamentable mischance, be destroyed or lost. There are many other reasons that appeal to the writer as arguments why the First Records of Baltimore Town should be given to the public; hence the public has them.

WILBUR F. COYLE,

BALTIMORE, December 1st, 1905.   *City Librarian.*

Explanatory Note

The contemplated publication of the First Records of Baltimore Town suggested also the printing of the Act which authorized the erection of Baltimore Town.

A copy of this was, happily, obtained at the State Library, and is given here just as it appears in the original.

Two other Acts, important links in the chain of historical events associated with early Baltimore, are also reproduced, to wit: An Act authorizing the "erection" of Jonas Town, later Jones' Town, on the North (generally referred to as East) bank of Jones' Falls, at the point where that stream is now spanned by Gay street bridge; and another which provided for the consolidation of Baltimore, and Jones' Town under the name of Baltimore Town.

Hence, this volume covers three distinct periods:

First—The "erection" of Baltimore Town—1729.

Second—The "erection" of Jonas (Jones) Town—1732.

Third—The consolidation of Baltimore and Jones Town as Baltimore Town—1745.

As stated, the Acts cited are so directly connected with the town's history and interwoven with the records herein given—in fact, lead up to the latter—that concurrent publication was deemed advisable.

The writer feels it will be generally appreciated that there is a great deal of important history represented by these three laws, and that they constitute a highly fitting and very desirable introduction to the publication of the town records.

Acts and records—taken together—say, as prologue and sequel—give, in their own way, a far better history along certain lines of very early Baltimore than can be written by any latter day individual.

It may be of some interest to note that meagre references to the Act authorizing Baltimore Town are to be found in the unprinted journals of the General Assembly of 1729, in the custody of the Maryland Historical Society. The bill may be traced from July 14th to August 8th, which latter date it was signed by the Governor of the Province. The archives show that "several inhabitants in and about Patapsco River and the rest of the inhabitants of Baltimore County" petitioned the General Assembly for authority to erect Baltimore Town. This petition was presented to the Upper House July 14th, 1729, was "read and recommended to the Consideration of the Lower House of Assembly with the further indorsement 'we the subscribers proprietors of the land mentioned in the within petition do consent there may an act pass as prayed for * * *

'CHARLES CARROLL,'
'DANIEL CARROLL.'"

On reading the petition in the Lower House it was "ordered that leave be given to bring in the bill prayed for." The next hint of the parliamentary progress of the Act is found later in the Upper House journal, as follows: "A bill from the Lower House by Mr. Mathews and Mr. Scott, entitled 'an act for erecting a Town on the North Side of the Patapsco River in Baltimore County' * * * indorsed by the Lower House of Assembly July 23rd, 1729 * * * was read a first and second time and will pass." This prophesy proved true. The journal shows the bill was signed August 8th, 1729, by the Governor, and became a law.   W. F. C.

Maps---Engravings

It is hoped the maps contained in this work will be interesting and useful, for it is not pretended that they are ornamental.

It is, likewise, not claimed that they improve the general appearance of the volume, but they can hardly help being of value taken in connection with the data given in print.

It was thought best to have the drawings made on a comprehensive scale; large enough to be of some real assistance to those who might consult them. They were made with the utmost care, and are copies of originals at the City Library.

The majority of lots referred to in these records may be easily located on the maps, and in this way the exact spot where first Baltimoreans reared their homes may be ascertained.

For lots located in later additions to Baltimore Town, that is, later than 1747, to which date the plats given bring the Town, maps at the City Library may be consulted.

The publication might, perhaps, have been made more attractive had illustrations of a certain class been used. This could easily have been done, and at little expense. Care, however, has been taken to disassociate this compilation with suggestions of a picture book.

There were available, and are yet in the custody of the City Librarian, various old prints of Baltimore which would have made an interesting display. Likewise, photographs of modern Baltimore would have added pictorial attractiveness to these pages, but the object sought, and the idea adhered to and developed has been, not to evolve a pictorial display, more or less fanciful, of old Baltimore, but to give to the public a collection of facts in as convenient form as possible, and to make absolutely certain that each fact is founded upon a "cut and dried" record which can be produced in the original at a moment's notice.

Hence, this is a record; not a picture book. It has been deemed no violation of this policy, that in order to further strengthen the idea of authenticity in the reader's mind, three photographic reproductions, taken from the First Book of Baltimore Town, have been used.

Other than this the suggestion (which at one time amounted to a temptation) to incorporate pictures, was put aside.

ACT OF 1729 AUTHORIZING "ERECTION" OF BALTIMORE TOWN.

AN ACT for erecting a Town on the North Side of Patapsco, in Baltemore County; and for laying out in Lots Sixty Acres of Land, in and about the place where one John Fleming now lives.

Whereas, several of the inhabitants of Baltemore County, have, by their Petition to this General Assembly, set forth, That a Town is much wanting on the North Side of Patapsco River; and that it is generally agreed, that Part of the Tract of Land, whereon a certain John Fleming now lives, and suppos'd to be the Right of the Heirs of Charles Carroll, Esq; decease'd; which said Tract is commonly Known by the Name of Cole's Harbour:

BE IT THEREFORE ENACTED, *by the Right Honourable the Lord Proprietary, by and with the Advice and Consent of His Lordship's Governour, and the Upper & Lower Houses of Assembly and the Authority of the same,* That Mr. Thomas Tolley, Mr. William Hamilton, Mr. William Bucknar, Doctor George Walker, Mr. Richard Giest, Doctor George Buchanan, Mr. William Hammond, or any Three of them, shall be, and are hereby appointed Commissioners for Baltemore County aforesaid; authorized and empowered, as well to agree for the Buying and Purchasing Sixty Acres of Land out of the Tract aforesaid, and such Part, not exceeding Sixty Acres, as lies most convenient to the Water, as for Surveying and Laying the Same out in the most convenient Manner into Sixty equal Lots, to be erected into a Town.

AND BE IT FURTHER ENACTED, That the Commissioners aforesaid, hereinbefore nominated and appointed, or the major Part of them, are hereby impowered sometime before the last Day of September which shall be in the Year of our Lord God, One thousand Seven Hundred and Thirty, to meet together on the Tract of Land aforesaid, or some other convenient Place thereto; and shall then and there treat and agree with the Owner or Owners, and Persons interested in the said Sixty Acres of Land, for the same; and after Pur-

chase thereof, shall cause the same to be surveyor and laid out;
and after the same to be so survey'd and laid out, shall cause
the same Sixty Acres to be mark'd, stak'd out, and divided
into convenient Streets, Lanes, and Allies, as near as may be
into Sixty equal Lots, mark'd by some Posts or Stakes towards
the Streets, or Lanes, with Number One, Two, Three, Four,
and so on to Sixty, to be divided and laid out; of which Lots
the Owner or Owners of the said Land shall have his or their
first Choice for one Lot; and after such Choice, the remaining
Lots may be taken up by others; and that no Person shall
presume to purchase more than One Lot within the said Sixty
Acres, during the first Four Months after laying out the same;
and that the said Lots shall be purchased by the Inhabitants
of the County aforesaid.

And in case the said Inhabitants shall not take up the said
Lots within Six Months after such laying out as aforesaid, it
shall then be lawful for any Person or Persons whatsoever to
take up the said Lot or Lots paying the Owner or Owners proportionably for the same. And in Case the Owner or Owners of
the aforesaid Sixty Acres of Land, shall wilfully refuse to
make Sale of the same, or that through Nonage, Coverture,
or any other disability or Impediment whatsoever, are disabled to make such Sale as aforesaid, that then the Commissioners aforesaid, or the major Part of them, shall, and are
by Virtue of this Act, authorized, impowered, and required,
to issue Warrants under their Hands and Seals, to the sheriff
of the said County; which said Sheriff is also hereby required
and empowered upon receipt of such Warrants, to impanel and
return a Jury of the most substantial Freeholders, Inhabitants
within the said County, to be and appear before the said Commissioners, at a certain Day and Time by them to be limited;
which Jury, upon their Oaths, shall enquire to whom the said
Land belongs, and assess and return what Damages and
Recompence they shall think fit to be awarded to the Owners
of the said Sixty Acres of Land, and all persons interested
therein, according to their several and respective interests:
And what Sum of Tobacco the said Jury shall adjudge the
said Sixty Acres to be worth, shall be paid to the Owners so
found by their Verdict, and all Persons they find interested
therein, by such Person or Persons as shall take up the said

Lots, proportionably to their Lot or Lots; which shall give the said Purchaser or Purchasers, their Heirs and assigns, an absolute Estate of Fee Simple, in the said Lot or Lots; he or they complying with the Requisites in this Act mentioned.

AND BE IT FURTHER ENACTED, That the Surveyor of Baltemore County, for the Time being, shall have and receive for Surveying and Laying out the Town aforesaid, the Sum of Fifteen Hundred Pounds of Tobacco, and no more, to be paid and allowed him in the County Levy; and that he return a Plat thereof to the County Clerk, to be by him kept amongst the County Records. And in Case the Taker-up of such Lot or Lots, refuse and neglect to build upon such Lot or Lots within Eighteen Months an House that shall cover Four Hundred square Feet; that then it shall and may be lawful for any other Person or Persons whatsoever, to enter upon the said Lot or Lots, so as aforesaid not built upon, paying such Sum of Tobacco as shall be first set and assessed upon such Lot to the Commissioners aforesaid, or such other Person as the said Commissioners, or the major Part of them, shall nominate and appoint to receive the same for the publick use and Benefit of the said Town, and to be taken up a second Time.

PROVIDED ALWAYS, That such Taker-up or Purchaser build and finish, within Eighteen Months after such his Entry made, such House as in this Act is before limited and appointed to be built by the first Taker-up; which House so built, shall give and settle as good Estates to all Intents and Purposes to such second Taker-up and Builder as aforesaid, his Heirs and Assigns as is in and by this Act before limited and settled upon the first Taker-up and Builder. And in Case any of the said Lots shall be neglected to be taken up in the Town aforesaid, during the Term of Seven Years next after the Publication of this Act, that then, and in such Case, the Owner or Persons interested at the first in such Land, shall, after such Time expired, be possess'd and interested in the said Lot or Lots, as in their first and former Estate: Any Thing in this Act to the contrary notwithstanding.

AND BE IT FURTHER ENACTED, *by the Authority aforesaid, by and with the Advice and Consent aforesaid,* That the Town aforesaid, be called by the name of Baltemore Town.

AND BE IT FURTHER ENACTED, *by the Authority aforesaid, by and with the Advice and Consent aforesaid,* That the Commissioners aforesaid, or the major Part of them, employ some sufficient Person for their Clerk; and that they cause such Clerk to take an Oath, that he shall make true and impartial Entries of their Proceedings; and assess reasonable Fees for the said Clerk, to be paid him by the several Takers-up of the said Lots; which said Entries they shall cause to be made up in a well bound Book, and lodged with the Clerk of Baltemore County Court, for the Inspection of any Person.

Saving to His Most Sacred Majesty, his Heirs and Successors, the Right Honourable the Lord Proprietary, his Heirs and Successors, and to all Bodies Politick and Corporate, and all Persons not mentioned in this Act, their several and respective Rights: Any Thing in this Act to the contrary thereof in anywise, notwithstanding

ACT OF 1732 AUTHORIZING "ERECTION" OF JONAS TOWN, LATER CALLED JONES TOWN, MERGED WITH BALTIMORE TOWN IN 1745.

AN ACT for erecting a Town on a Creek, divided on the East, from the Town lately laid out in Baltimore County, called Baltimore Town, on the Land whereon Edward Fell Keeps Store.

Be it Enacted, by the Right Honourable the Lord Proprietary by and with the Advice and Consent of his Lordship's Governor and the Upper and Lower Houses of Assembly, and the Authority of the same, That Mr. Thomas Sheredine, Mr. John Cockey, Mr. Robert North, Capt. John Boring, and Mr. Thomas Todd, or any Three of them, shall be and are hereby appointed Commissioners for Baltimore County aforesaid, and are hereby authorized, and impowered, as well to agree for the buying and purchasing Ten Acres of Land out of the Tract aforesaid, and such Part, not exceeding Ten Acres, as lies most convenient to the Water, as for surveying and laying out the same, in the most convenient Manner, into Twenty equal Lots, to be erected into a Town.

And be it further Enacted, That the Commissioners aforesaid herein before nominated and appointed, or the major Part of them, are hereby empowered, some Time before the Thirtieth Day of November, which shall be in the Year of our Lord God, One Thousand Seven Hundred and Thirty Two, to meet together on the Tract of Land aforesaid, or some other convenient Place adjoining thereto, and then and there treat and agree with the Owner or Owners, and Persons interested in the said Ten Acres of Land, for the same; and after Purchase thereof, shall cause the same to be surveyed, laid out, and divided, as near as may be, into Twenty equal Lots, allowing such sufficient Space or Quantity thereof, for Streets, Lanes, and Alleys, as to them shall seem meet, with Posts or Stakes towards every Street, Lane, or Alley, the said Lots to be numbered One, Two, Three, and so on to Twenty, for the better and more sure distinguishing each Lot from the other; of which Twenty Lots, the Owner or Owners

of the said Land, shall have his or their first Choice for One
Lot; and after such Choice, the remaining Lots may be taken
up by others: And that no Person shall presume to purchase
more than One Lot within the said Ten Acres, during the first
Four Months after laying out the same; and that the said Lots
shall be purchased by the Inhabitants of the County aforesaid: And in Case the said Inhabitants shall not take up the
said Lots within Six Months after such laying out, as aforesaid, it shall then be lawful for any Person or Persons whatsoever, to take up the said Lot or Lots, paying the Owners or
Owners proportionably for the same. And in Case the Owner
or Owners of the aforesaid Ten Acres, shall wilfully refuse to
make sale of the same; or that through Nonage, Coverture,
or other Disability or Impediment whatsoever, are disabled to
make such Sale, as aforesaid, That then the Commissioners
aforesaid, or the major Part of them, shall and are by Virtue
of this Act, authorized, empowered, and required, to issue Warrants under their Hands and Seals to the Sheriff of the said
County; which said Sheriff is also hereby required and empowered, upon receipt of such Warrants, to empanel and return a Jury of the most substantial Freeholders, Inhabitants
within the said County, to be and appear before the said Commissioners, at a certain Day and Time by them to be limited:
Which Jury, upon their Oaths, shall enquire to whom the said
Land belongs, and assess and return what Damages and
recompence they shall think fit to be awarded to the Owners
of the said Ten Acres of Land, and to all Persons interested
therein, according to their several and respective interests.
And what Sum of Tobacco the said Jury shall adjudge the
said Ten Acres of Land to be worth shall be paid to the Owners so found by their Verdict, and to all Persons they find interested therein, by such Person or Persons as shall take up
the said Lots, proportionably to their Lot or Lots; which shall
give the said Purchaser or Purchasers, their Heirs and Assigns, an absolute Estate of Fee Simple in the said Lot or
Lots, he or they complying with the Requisites in this Act
mentioned.

And be it further Enacted, That the Surveyor of Baltimore
County, for the Time being, shall have and receive for surveying and laying out the Town aforesaid, the sum of Four

Hundred Pounds of Tobacco, and no more, to be paid and allowed him in the County Levy; and that he return a Plat thereof to the County Clerk to be by him Kept amongst the County Records. And in Case the Taker-up of such Lot or Lots refuse or neglect to build upon such Lot or Lots, with Eighteen Months, an House that shall cover Four Hundred Square Feet, that then it shall and may be lawful for any other Person or Persons whatsoever, to enter upon the said Lot or Lots, so as aforesaid not built upon, paying such Sum of Tobacco as shall be first set and assessed upon such Lot, to the Commissioners aforesaid, or such other Person as the said Commissioners, or the major Part of them, shall nominate and appoint to receive the same for the Publick Use and Benefit of the said Town, and to be taken upon a Second Time.

Provided always, That such Taker-up or Purchaser build and finish, within Eighteen months after such his Entry made, such House, as in this Act is before limited and appointed to be built by the first Taker-up; which House so built, shall give and settle as good an Estate, to all Intents and Purposes, to such second Taker-up and Builder, as aforesaid, his Heirs and Assigns, and is in and by this Act before limited and settled upon the first Taker-up and Builder. And in Case any of the said Lots shall be neglected to be taken up in the Town aforesaid, during the term of Seven Years next after the Publication of this Act, that then, and in such Case, the Owner, or Persons interested at first in such Land, shall, after such Time expired, be possessed and interested in the said Lot or Lots as in their first and former Estate; anything in this Act to the contrary notwithstanding.

And be it enacted, by the Authority aforesaid, by and with the Advice & Consent aforesaid, That the Town aforesaid be called by the Name of Jonas Town.

And be it further Enacted, by the Authority aforesaid, by and with the Advice and Consent aforesaid That the Commissioners aforesaid, or the major Part of them, employ some sufficient Person for their Clerk; and that they cause such Clerk to take an Oath, that he shall make true and impartial Entries of their Proceedings, and assess reasonable Fees for the said Clerk, to be paid him by the several Takers-up of the said Lots; which said Entries they shall cause to be made

upon a well bound book, and lodged with the Clerk of Baltimore County Court, for the Inspection of any Person.

Saving to his most Sacred Majesty, his Heirs and Successors, the Right Honourable the Lord Proprietary, his Heirs
and Successors, and to all Bodies Politick and Corporate, and
all Persons not mentioned in this Act, their several and respective Rights; anything in this Act to the contrary thereof,
in any-wise notwithstanding.

*And be it further Enacted, by the Authority, Advice and
Consent aforesaid,* That every Person taking up, or being in
Possession of any of the Lots taken up in the aforesaid Town,
shall be chargeable with, and liable to the Payment of One
Penny Current Money of Maryland, per annum, for each Lot,
to the Right Honourable the Lord Proprietary, and his Heirs
forever; and that the Clerk of the said Commissioners do trans-
mit to his Lordship's Agent, an Account of all Lots taken up,
pursuant to the Directions of this Act.

ACT OF 1745 BY VIRTUE OF WHICH BALTIMORE AND JONES TOWNS WERE CONSOLIDATED UNDER NAME OF BALTIMORE TOWN.

A supplementary and Additional Act Entituled, An Act for erecting a Town on the North side of Patapsco, in Baltimore County; and for laying out in Lots Sixty acres of Land, in and about the Place where John Fleming now lives: And to an Act entituled, An Act for erecting a Town on a Creek divided on the East from the Town lately laid out in Baltimore County, called Baltimore-Town, on the Land whereon Edward Fell Keeps store.

Whereas, the Inhabitants of Baltimore and Jone's Towns, in the County of Baltimore, have, by their humble Petition to this General Assembly, set forth, that the said Towns are very conveniently situated in regard to the back Inhabitants, and Navigation on the Head of the North-West Branch of Patapsco River, and only parted by the Head of the said Branch, over which they have erected a good Bridge, which makes a very easy Communication between them, And proves greatly to the Service, not only of the said Town, but Travellers in general: As also that the said Towns, in regard that they are so contiguous to each other, the same might be reduced into one Town, by the name of Baltimore Town; that the several Boundaries, which at present are not, may be well ascertained; and

Preamble.

that Commissioners may be appointed, in order
to fully to execute this Act, and see the said Towns
carefully surveyed. And further they set forth,
that there are several Sums of Money due from
Takers-up of Lots in the said Town, in virtue of
the several Laws whereby the said Towns were
erected, and that the Commissioners to be appointed by this Act may have Power to receive
and recover the same, to be applied to the Use of
the said Town; and also that the Commissioners
to be appointed by this Act may have Succession.
They further set forth, that several Lots in the
said Towns were not taken up under the former
Laws, but that some have since been purchased
from the Owners of said Towns; and that it is
highly probable all the Lots in the said Towns,
not yet taken up or purchased, in a very short
Time will. Therefore they humbly pray, that
such as have already purchased, or may hereafter
purchase Lots, within the original Survey of said
Towns, may to all Intents and Purposes have and
enjoy, as sure and indefeasible Estates in Fee-
Simple, in the said Lots so purchased, or to be
purchased, as if the said Lots had been taken up
and improved according to the Direction of the
Laws that erected the said Towns; and that all
Improvements, that are or may be made out of
the Water, be secured to the Improver or Improvers, as fully and amply, as if the same had
been originally laid out within the Bounds of the
said Towns. And further they pray, that no
Swine, Sheep, or Geese may be kept or raised
within said Town, unless kept in Inclosures. All

which this General Assembly think reasonable
to be Enacted.

Be it therefore Enacted by the Right Honourable the Lord Proprietary, by and with the Advice
and Consent of his Lordship's Governor, and the
Upper and Lower Houses of Assembly, and the
Authority of the same, That the same Towns, now
called Baltimore and Jone's Town, be incorporated
into one entire Town, and for the future called and
known by the name of Baltimore-Town, and by
no other name, and that the Bridge the inhabitants
of said Town have built on the Branch that
divided said Towns, be for the future deemed a
public Bridge, repaired and kept passable for
Man, Horse, Cart, or Wagon, for the future at
the Expense and charge of Baltimore County.

The two towns to be incorporated into one town.

And be it further Enacted, That Major
William Hammond, Capt. Robt. North, Capt.
Thomas Sheredine, Dr. George Buchanan, Col.
William Hammond, Capt. Robert North, Capt.
Darby Lux, Mr. Thomas Harrison, and Mr. William Fell, be and are hereby appointed Commissioners, in order to see this present Act, and the
former Acts relating to the Towns before mentioned, put in Execution; and that they cause the
said Towns, to be carefully surveyed by the Out-
Lines of said Towns, and therein include the
Branch over which the Bridge is built; and that
they from time to time cause all the Lots taken up
and improved, or that hereafter shall be taken up
and improved, to be regularly surveyed, substan-
tially and fairly bounded, and numbered, in order

Commissioners appointed for the said Towns.

to prevent any Disputes that may happen touching the Right to any the said Lots, or any Part
of them.

And be it further Enacted by the Authority
aforesaid, That when and as often as any of the
said Commissioners shall die, remove out of the
County, or decline and refuse to act as Commissioner, that then the major Part of the Commissioners for the Time being shall, in the Room
of such Commissioner, appoint and nominate
another to serve, in the Stead of such Commission so dying, removing or refusing to serve.
And that should any Dispute hereafter arise,
touching the Bounds of any Lot or Lots within
the same Town, that the same shall be fully determined by the said Commissioners, or the major
Part of them: And to prevent any Partiality that
may be used therein, that the said Commissioners
or the major Part of them, meet at least once a
Year, and then see that a Boundary to each Lot
be kept up and preserved in Manner before prescribed; and in case any be decayed, that they
cause other sufficient Boundary to be fixed in the
Room of any missing or decayed.

And forasmuch that this, and other Matters in
this Act contained, will greatly tend to the Security of the Inhabitants of said Town, and the
Preservation of their Rights; Be it also Enacted,
That the said Commissioners have Power, by this
Act, to employ a Clerk, who shall be under Oath,
fairly and honestly to enter in a Book, to be kept
for that Purpose, all the Proceedings of said Com-

missioners relating to said Town; in which Book,
amongst other Things, shall be kept a fair Plat of
said Town, neatly platted, describing every Lot,
by its right Number, and who the Taker-up was
or shall be; and that all or any the said Commissioners, and their successors, shall have Recourse
to the Clerk's Book or Books, as frequently as
he or they please, without Fee or Reward, the
better to prevent any Corruption.

But in regard the Clerk and Surveyor, for their
Trouble, must have some Reward, Be it Enacted,
That the said Commissioners, or the major Part
of them, may levy, assess, and take by way of Dis-
tress if needful, from the Inhabitants of said
Town, by even and equal Proportion, the sum of
three Pounds yearly for the Encouragement of
their Clerk, to be paid to him, and that they have
Power to place and displace their Clerk as often
as they shall think fit: And that the County-Court
of Baltimore have Power, and hereby are required, at the Request of said Commissioners, or
the major Part of them, to levy on the taxable
Inhabitants of said County, any sum not exceeding fifteen hundred Pounds of Tobacco, for the
Use of the Surveyor, or Person that shall be employed in surveying and laying out the said Town.

Surveyors & Clerk's Fees.

And whereas it is suggested there are sundry
sums of Money, due and owing to the first Commissioners nominated for said Towns, from several Takers-up of Lots in said Towns, under the
original Laws for laying them out; Be it Enacted,
That the present Commissioners and their suc-

Money due on Lots formerly taken up, to be recovered by the Com-missioners.

cessors or the major Part of them, may by due Course of Law, or in any other Legal Manner, in the name of the said Commissioners, or the major Part of them, take, demand, receive, and recover the same, wherever any Sum of Money, by virtue of the original Laws for laying out said Towns, shall be found due; which said Commissioners, or the major Part of them, shall apply to the Uses intended by the said original Law for laying out the said Towns and in no other Manner.

Concerning After Purchasers & c.

And whereas there are several Lots within the Limits of said Towns, and the Out Bounds of them, untaken up, and that hereafter may be purchased from the Proprietors of said Lands; Be it Enacted, that all After Purchasers shall be deemed to be within said Town, and that such After Purchasers, whether before or after the making of this Act, shall be deemed to be within the said Town; provided their Lots shall be within the Out Lines of said Town; and have as good Estate in their Lots, as if taken up, improved, and paid for, under the original Laws erecting said Towns.

Improvements made out of the Water.

And be it further Enacted by the Authority aforesaid, That all Improvements of what kind soever, Either Wharfs, Houses, or other Buildings, that have, or shall be made out of the Water, or where it usually flows, as an Encouragement to such Improvers, be forever deemed the Right, Title, and Inheritance of such Improver or Improvers, their Heirs and Assigns for ever.

And be it further Enacted by the Authority
aforesaid, That it shall not hereafter be lawful
for any Person or Persons whatsoever, to keep or
raise any Swine, Sheep, or Geese, within the said
Town, unless they be well inclosed in some Lot
or Pen.

No swine,
sheep & c, to
be raised in
said Town.

And whereas there are several very valuable
Improvements made in said Towns, by Virtue of
the Laws already made, and whereby they were
erected into Towns; Be it Enacted by the Authority aforesaid, by and with the Advice and Consent aforesaid. That all Takers-up of Lots, and
former and after Purchasers under this or the
former Laws, complying with the Requisites
directed by such former Laws and this, shall have
a sure and indefeasible Estate of Inheritance in
Fee Simple in said Lots taken up by him or them;
any Law, Usage, or Custom, to the contrary notwithstanding

On the following page begin the actual records of the town, to wit: the minutes of the First meeting of the Commission which selected the site for Baltimore.

Except in one instance, headings, foot notes, and marginal annotations have been omitted in order that the printed pages might conform as nearly as possible to the originals. Throughout this book the name of the new town is spelled two ways —Baltemore and Baltimore. The former mode is not only peculiar to the records themselves, up to a certain point, but appears also in the original legislative act authorizing the "erection" of the town. In the course of compilation, however, when it became necessary to write the name—as in the title, or in a headline, the more modern form of spelling was employed.

Fol: 1.

On Munday the first day of Decr. 17
the following Commissioners viz.

Mess.rs {
Richd: Gist
William Hamilton
George Buchanan
George Walker
}

being four of the Seven Commissioners appoin
by Act of Assembly for agreeing wth. Charles Carr
& Daniel Carroll Esqs about the price & purchase o
Sixty Acres of land to be erected into a Town call
Baltemore-Town and the said four Commissioners
agreed with the said Charles Carroll Esqs on
own behalf & on behalf of his brother Daniel then
absent to pay them the said Charles & Daniel or the
order the sume of forty shillings current money of Mary
or else tobacco to be paid in the hands of the Sherif of
Baltemore County at one penny p th until it amou
to forty shillings value p Acre to be paid by each Pur
=aser of a Lott in the sd Town to the said Charles & Dan
or their heirs & Assignes.
The same day the said Commissioners appointed the sec
Munday of January being the 12th day of Jany next to
meet the Surveyor of Baltemore County on the Tract of
land call'd Cole's Harbour; which is the land pitch'd up
by the Assembly for the erection of Baltemore Town t
on, and there to give him the said Surveyor direction
for laying out the said Town.

On the 12th day of January 172 9/30 then the foll
Commissioners for Baltemore Town &c. on

On Munday the first day of Decr: 1729 met the following
Commissioners viz.   RICHD: GIST

Messrs.   WILLIAM HAMILTON
            GEORGE BUCHANAN
            GEORGE WALKER

being four of the Seven Commissioners appointed by Act of
Assembly for agreeing wth Charles Carroll & Daniel Carroll
Esqs about the price & purchase of Sixty Acres of land to be
erected into a Town called Baltemore-Town and the said four
Commissioners agreed with the said Charles Carroll Esqs on
his own behalf & on behalf of his brother Daniel then absent to
pay them the said Charles & Daniel or their order the sume of
forty shillings current money of Maryland or else tobacco to be
paid in the hands of the Sherrif of Baltemore County at one
penny p ℔ until it amount to forty shillings value p Acre to
be paid by each Purchaser of a lott in the sd Town to the said
Charles & Daniel or their heirs & Assignes.

The same day the said Commissioners appointed the second
Munday of January being the 12th day of Janry: next to meet
the Surveyor of Baltemore County on the Tract of land call'd
Cole's Harbour; which is the land pitch'd upon by the Assembly for the erection of Baltemore Town afc on, and there
to give him the said Surveyor directions for laying out the
said Town.

On the 12th day of January 1729/30 then the following
Commissioners for Baltemore Town mett on the Tract of land
call'd Cole's Harbour, on which the said Town was design'd,
viz.   WILLIAM BUCKNER
            WILLIAM HAMMOND

Messrs: RICHARD GIST
            GEORGE BUCHANAN
            GEORGE WALKER

and there ordered the Surveyor of Baltemore County to Runn
out the Town aforsaid Begining at a Locust post to be sett up
on a point of the said land and running—from the sd Locust
post East 5½ perches, North 21° East 10 p. North East 19 p.
North 69° East 12 p. North 72° 30' East 22 p. South 55° East
14 p. South 75° East 18 p. South 53° 30' East 6 p. North 86
p. West 14 p. South 6 p. West 14 p. South 4 p. West 18 p.
North 69° West 22 North 20° West 26 p. South 40° West 46 p.

South 50° West 32 p. South 30° West 23 p. South 41° 30' East 17 p. then to the begining Locust post. containing Sixty Acres of land to be divided into sixty Lotts with convenient streets & lanes.

On the same day the said Commissioners appointed George Walker, being one of their Number, for their Clerk; who the following day was qualified befor Mr Richd Gist by taking ane oath to make true & impartial enteries of the proceedings of the Commissioners for Baltemore Town, as also the taking up the Lotts thereof.

On Wedensday the 14th day of January 1729/30 these Lotts were taken up as follows, by the underwritten Gentlemen who secur'd their titles to the same by begining & finish on their Respective Lotts houses that covered at least four hundred square feet of ground (as was required of the takers up of Lotts by act of Assembly) within less than eighteen months after their taking them up. viz.

Lotts taken up in
Balt: Town

No: 49		CHARLES CARROLL ESQR...No: 49:
37		PHILIP JONES JUNR..... 37:
38		JAMES JACKSON......... 38:
52		GEORGE WALKER........ 52:
48	Messrs	RICHARD GIST.......... 48:
45		WILLIAM HAMMOND..... 45:
55		MORDECAI PRICE........ 55:
56		CHRISTOPHER GIST...... 56:

Memorandum that the above named Mordecai Price convey'd his right and title to the above Lott No: 55 to Capt Robert Gordon of Annapolis & his heirs for ever who comply'd with the requisites mentioned in the Act of Assembly for Baltemore Town.

James Jackson also convey'd his right to ye Lott No: 38 unto Mr Samuel Peel & his heirs who duly comply'd wth sd requisites.

+ On Thursday the 15th of January 1729/30 the three following lotts were taken up by the underwritten Gentlemen but they forfeited their right thereto by not building thereupon as required by Act of Assembly.

No: 44   { THOMAS SHEREDINE.............44:
53   Messrs: { WILLIAM BUCKNER...............53:
26   { JAMES POWELL..................26:

+   On Friday ye 16th of January 1729/30 the two following Lotts were taken up by the following Gentlemen viz

No: 54   Messrs: { CHARLES RIDGELY................54:
36   { LUKE TROTTEN...................36:

Sometime afterward the said Ridgely convey'd the sd Lott No: 54 to Mr John Diggs who built upon the same as required by Act of Assembly in due time.

The above sd Luke Trotten also convey'd his right to The sd Lott No: 36 unto Mr Philip Jones junr: who comply'd with the Requistes of the Act of Assembly.

+   On Munday the 19th of January 1729/30 the two following Lotts were taken up by the underwritten Gentlemen who forfited their right thereto by not building thereupon viz

No: 10   CAPT ROBT NORTH.................10
35   RICHARD HEWITT..................35

On the same day Mr Lloyd Harris took up the Lott
50   No: 50 and fully comply'd with the requisites in the Act of Assembly in due time.

+   On Tuesday following being the 20th day of January 1729/30 Capt Thomas Sheredine took up the
No: 14   Lott No: 14 in the name & for the use of his Son Daniel Sheredine but suffer'd their right thereto to become void for want of building thereon as by Act of Assembly enjoyn'd.

+   On Wednesday being the 21st of January 1729/30
No: 51   Mr Lloyd Harris took up the Lott No: 56 in the name of John Gorsuch which Gorsuch afterwards convey'd his right thereto unto the sd Lloyd Harris which sd Harris built upon as required by Act of Assembly.

+   Aprile 18: 1730 David Robinson took up in Bal-
No: 47   temore town the Lott No: 47 & afterwards convey'd his right thereto unto Mr Richard Gist who built thereon as by Act of Assembly required.

+   July 1: 1730 Mr John Risteau took the Lott
No: 15 No: 15 in Baltemore town and built thereon ane house
that was deem'd to cover four hundred square feet
of ground within the time prescribed by Act of Assembly.

+   Augt 18: 1730 Mr William Hammond took up
No: 46 the Lott No: 46 in Baltemore town but neglected to
build thereon in eighteen months time but took it
up a second for which second purchase of the said
Lott he is Debtor to the sd town as order'd by Act of
Assembly

+   March 1st 1730/1 Martine Parlett took up the
No: 42 Lott No: 42 in Baltemore town & forfeited his right
thereto by neglecting to build thereon.

+   February 22: 1730/1 Then the Vestry of St.
Paul's Parrish in Baltemore County took up the Lott
No: 19 No: 19 in the above sd town to build the church of .
St Paul's Parrish on.

+   Aprile 30: 1731 Then Docr: James Walker of
No: 9 Ann Arundell County took up the Lott No: 9 in Baltemore town & secur'd his title thereto by building
thereon as by Act of Assembly prescrib'd.

+   July 16: 1731 George Walker took up the Lott
No: 53 No: 53 which had been taken up by Mr William
Buckner on the 15th of January 1729/30 but was not
built upon by the sd Buckner within eighteen months
as by law prescrib'd but was built upon by the sd
Walker in the limited time after the second taking up.

+   November 5: 1731 Then Mr John Giles took up
No: 39 a Lott in Baltemore town No: 39 which he let fall
again by neglecting to build thereon.

+   May 12th: 1732 Then Mr Richd: Lewis took up
No: 11 a Lott in Baltemore town No: 11 and paid forty
shillings being the purchase money thereof.

+   May 20th 1732 Then Mr Richard Gist took up a
No: 59 Lott in Baltemore town No 59 and paid the purchase
money thereof.

+   June 28: 1734 Then the Revrd Mr Joseph Hooper
No: 22 took up a Lott in Baltemore town No: 22

+   July 3: 1734 Then the above the sd the Reverd

No : 44   Mr Joseph Hooper took up the Lott No: 44 which was taken up formerly by Capt Thomas Sheredine on the 15th. of January 1729/30

+

No : 39   August 8: 1734 Then Mr Thomas Woodward took up the Lott No 39 in Baltemore Town and paid the Consideration for the same in paper Currancy of Maryland.

No : 16

+

21   Septr: 16: 1734 Then the Revrd Mr Joseph Hooper took up two Lotts in Baltemore town viz No: 16 and 21

+

No : 43   March 4th: 1734/5 Then came John Smith Cooper in Baltemore County by his Proxy Mr Richard Gist and took up a Lott in Baltemore Town No: 43 and paid the purchase money & fees thereof.

+

No : 10   March 28th: 1735 Then came Mr Joshua Hall joyner in Baltemore County & took up a Lott in Baltemore town No: 10: which was on the 19th of January 1729/30 taken up by Capt. Robert North but was not built upon by the said North as required by Act of Assembly & the foresd Hall paid the purchase money & the fee thereof.

+

No : 42   November 21: 1735 Then the Revrd Mr Joseph Hooper took up the Lott No: 42 in Baltemore town in the name & for the sole use & behoof of the Revrd Mr John Humphreys & his heirs.

+

No : 44   January 19: 1735/6 Then the Revrd Mr Joseph Hooper having neglected to build within the time appointed by Law upon the Lott No: 44 which he had taken up formerly viz on the 3d of July 1734 desir'd that the same Lott No: 44 might be a second time entered in his name and for his use.

+

No : 40   January 23: 1735/6 Then came Mr Thomas Woodward in the name and on behalf of Capt Francis Kipps and took up the Lott No: 40 in Baltemore town and paid the purchase money thereof.

+

No : 41   January 23: 1735/6 Then came Mr Thomas Woodward in the name and on behalf of Mr Gideon Donaldson and took up the Lott No: 41 in Baltemore town and paid the purchase money thereof.

+   Janry: 27: 1736/7 Then came Mr Joshua Hall who having neglected to build in the time limited by

No: 10 Law upon his Lott No: 10 in Baltemore Town and
desired the said Lott might be reentered in his name
& for his use which now is accordingly done.

+   March 4: 1737/8 Then Mr Joshua Hall came &
No: 14 order'd the Lott No: 14 in Baltemore Town which
was taken up by Capt Thomas Sheredine on the 20th
day of Janry 1729/30 in the name of his son Daniel
to be enter'd in his name & for his use for ever.
N. B. He the sd Hall paid the purchase & fees
thereof.

+   March 4th 1737/8 Then came Mr William Rogers
No: 42 & desired that the Lotts 42: 43: & 44 in Baltemore
43   Town might be enter'd in his own name & for his
44   own use through the Default of the former Uptakers
thereof and the sd Rogers paid the purchase & the
fees thereof viz. the above sd three Lotts in Baltemore Town.

+   May 23: 1740 Then came Mr Edward Fotterell
& represented that he was apprehensive that the
No: 11 Lott No: 11: formerly viz: on the 12th of May 1732
taken up by Mr Richd Lewis became vacant & fell to
the use of Baltemore Town notwithstanding the sd
Lewis built a house upon the same which was re-
mov'd from off the sd Lott befor the doors were putt
up by Solomon Wooden the builder & the sd Fotterell
desires the sd Lott No: 11: may be entered in the
Register in his own name & for his own use (& he
promises to pay the Commissioners for the same)
which is now accordingly done.

+   July 23: 1740 Then Mr Wm Rogers came & represented to me Clk: of Baltemore town that he was
No: 14 apprehensive that the the Lott No: 14 in sd town
formerly viz on the 20th day of January 1729/30
taken up by Capt Thos: Sheredine in the name and
on behalf of his son Daniel & afterward taken up on
the 4th day of March 1737/8 by Mr Joshua Hall who
has neglected to build thereon within eighteen months
after his taking up the same whereby the said Rogers
is apprehensive that the sd Lott again falls vacant for
the use of the said Town which he the sd Rogers de-

sires may be Registred in his own name which now
is done & he obliges himself & his heirs to satisfie the
Commissioners of sd Town for the same.

+ July 23: 1740 Then Mr Wm Rogers came and
represented that having formerly viz on the 4th of
No: 42 March 1737/8 taken up the Lott No 42 but neglected
building thereon within eighteen months as required
by act of assembly whereupon he desires the sd Lott
No 42 may be reentered in his own name which is
now done & he oblidges himself & his heirs to satisfie
the Commissioners of the sd town for the same.

+ Aprile 8: 1741 Then came Mr Edward Fottrell
No: 40 and desir'd that the Lotts No: 40 & 41 which were
41 formerly viz on Janr: 23: 1735/6 taken up by
Thomas Woodward in the name & for the use of
Messrs Francis Kipps & Gideon Donaldson may be
enter'd in his own name which is now done & he
obliges himself to satisfie the Commissioners of the
said town for the same.

| May 15: 1741 Then came ye Revrd Benedict
Bourdillon and desired the two following Lotts in
No: 26 Baltemore town viz No: 26: formerly taken up on the
15th day of Janry 1729/30 by James Powell and
35 No: 35: taken up by Richd Hewitt on ye 19th of
Janry: 1729/30 both unbuilt upon according to the
Directions of ye Act of Assembly by the sd Powell &
Hewitt may be enterd in his own name which is now
accordingly done & he obliges himself to satisfie the
Commissioners of the sd: town for both the sd Lotts.

+ Septr 24: 1741 Then came Mr. Edward Fottrell
& represented to the Clerk of Baltemore Town that
No: 39 the Lott No: 39 which was enter'd in the name of
Thomas Woodward on the 8th of August 1734 was
still vacant by reason the sd Woodward had not built
his house upon the said Lott but on ane other adjoyn-
ing wherefor the said Fottrell desir'd it might be enter'd in his own name & for his own use which is now
accordingly done & he the said Edward Fottrell
promises & obliges himself & his heirs to satisfie the
Commissioners of the said town for the sd Lott.

+   Decr: 22: 1741 Then came Mr Wm Rogers & represented to the Clerk of Baltemore town that whereas he hath neglected to build upon the Lott
No: 42   No: 42 as required by Act of Assembly which sd Lott was formerly viz: on ye 23 of July 1740 enter'd in ye name of the said Rogers & being apprehensive that because of that neglect his right to the sd Lott might be render'd precarious he therefor desires the sd Lott No: 42: might be enter'd in the Register in his own name which now is accordingly done & the sd Rogers promises & obliges himself & his heirs to satisfie the Commissioners of the sd town for the sd Lott.

+   Octobr: 15: 1742 Then the Revrd: Benedict: Bourdillon came & represented to me the Clerk of
No: 40   Baltemore town that whereas the two Lotts No:40:41:
41   formerly taken up by Kipps & Donaldson, now fall vacant they having not built thereon as p Act of Assembly, wherefor the sd Bourdillon requests that the said two Lotts No: 40: 41: may be enter'd in his own name & obliges himself & heirs to satisfie the Comssrs or any other propper person for the same which is now accordingly done.

+   March 4, 1742/3 Then came the Reverend Benedict Bourdillon and desired the two following Lotts
No. 26   in Baltemore town viz No 26 formerly taken up on
35   the 15th Janry 1729/30 by James Powell and No 35 taken up by Richard Hewitt Janry 19th 1729/30 both unbuilt upon according to the Directions of the Act of Assembly by said Powell and Hewitt, formerly taken up by said Bourdillon viz May 15: 1741 But not built upon and now desires that the said two Lotts may be again enter'd in the Register in his own name which is now done and obliges himself & his heirs to satisfye the Commissioners of the said town for the said two Lotts.

+   September 16. 1747. Came Doctr. George Buchanan Colo. William Hammond Capt. Darby Lux and Mr. Thomas Harrison desiring that the Lott in Baltimore

No. 26 Town No 26 first taken up by James Powell on the 15 Jany. 1729/30 afterwards by the Revd. Mr. Benedict Bourdillon twice Viz. first on the 15 May 1741, and then on March 4, 1742/3 now being forfeited for not Building thereon according to Act of Assembly, desire it may be entered in their Names each an equal

No 21 share. Also the Lott No 21, taken up the Sixteenth of Septemr. 1734 by the Revd. Mr. Joseph Hooper,

No. 22 Likewise the Lott No 22 taken up the 28 June 1734 by the Revd. Mr. Joseph Hooper which two Lotts being forfeited by neglecting to Build thereon according to Act of Assembly, they also desire that the said two Lotts may be also entered in their Names

No 39 each an equal share— Also the Lott No 39 taken up first by John Giles on the 5th Novemr. 1731 afterwards by Thomas Woodward on the 8th of August 1734. afterwards by Edward Fottrell on the 24 of September 1741,.—which Lot being forfeited for not Building thereon according to Act of Assembly desire may be entered in their Names each an equal share.

+ September the 26. 1747. Mr. Joseph Tayler came and representing to me William Lux Clerk of Balti-

No. 5 more Town that the Lott No. 5. in the said Town in that part formerly Jones's Town formerly taken up by Thomas Bond on July 20. 1733 afterwards by Mary Hanson on April 8. 1740 is become Vacant by not Building thereon according to Act of Assembly and desires the said Lott may be entered in the Name of Edward Fell son of Willm.

No. 6 And also the Lott No 6. in Jones's Town taken up by Willm. Fell on July 20. 1733 afterwards by Mary Hanson on April 8. 1740 is also become forfeited by not Building thereon according to Act of Assembly requests me the said Clerk to enter the same in the Name of Ann Fell which is now accordingly done.

Receiv'd Feby. 18. 1744 in Order to be Recorded
                              P BREREWOOD *Ck.*

+
1732
October 28

On the 28th day of October 1732 Capt. Thomas Sheredine, Capt Robert North, Mr Thomas Todd, and Mr John Cockey four of the Commissioners for a new town call'd Jones's Town to be erected on the East side ot Jones's Falls on a Tract of land called Cole's Harbour mett at a place near & convenient to the said Land and qualified George Walker to be their Clerk for the sd Town by administering to him ane oath to make true and impartial Enteries of their proceedings according to ane act of Assembly Enacted July 1732. At the same time also the sd four Commissioners issued their warrant, under their hands & seals; to the Sheriff of Baltemore County to summon a Jury of the most substantial freeholders of sd County to appear befor them on the sd Land called Cole's Harbour to inquire who is the Owner of the sd Land and to assess what they think tenn Acres of the same whereon the sd Town is to be erected is worth.

+
1732
November 4

1732
Novr: 4

On the 4th day of November 1732 Capt. Thomas Sheredine, Capt Robert North, Capt John Cockey, Capt John Boreing, & Mr Thomas Todd all the Commissioners appointed by Act of Assembly for laying out a Town convenient to the water, on a Tract of Land called Cole's Harbour: mett on the sd Land, and askt a certain William Fell, who is in present possession of the sd land; whither he would sell tenn Acres of land, out of the sd Tract; who answer'd positively, that he neither could nor would sell any of it; whereupon a jury of substantial freeholders, return'd by the Sherif

★ **Jones Town records begin on this page and end at page 17.**

On the 28th day of October 1732. Capt Thomas
Sheredine, Capt Robert North, Mr Thomas Tod
and Mr John Cockey four of the Commissioners for
a new town call'd Jones's Town to be erected on
the East side of Jones's Falls on a Tract of Land
called Cole's Harbour mett at a place near & convenient to the said Land and qualified George
Walker to be their Clerk for the sd Town by
administering to him ane oath to make true and
impartial Enteries of their proceedings according to
ane act of Assembly Enacted July 1732. At the
same time also the sd four Commissioners issued their
warrant, under their hands & seals; to the Sheriff of
Baltemore County to summon a Jury of the most
substantial freeholders of sd County to appear before
them on the sd Land called Cole's Harbour to inquire
who is the Owner of the sd Land and to assess what
they think tenn acres of the same whereon the
sd Town is to be erected is worth.

On the 4th day of November 1732 Capt Thomas
Sheredine, Capt Robert North, Capt John Cockey,
Capt John Boreing, & Mr Thomas Tod, all the Commissioners appointed &

1732 October 28

1732 November 4

FIRST MEETING OF COMMISSION WHICH SELECTED A TEN-ACRE SITE
FOR JONES' TOWN, OCTOBER 28TH, 1732.
(*Photographed from original.*)

of Baltemore County, proceeded (being first sworne by the sd Commissioners) to inquire who is Owner of sd Lands: and found by their Verdict the Orphan's of Coll Richd: Colegate decsd to be Owners of the sd Land, and judg'd the value of it, to be three hundred pounds of tobacco per Acre, for tenn acres thereof. At the same time also Mr Philip Jones Surveyor of Baltemore County, who was then & there present, began to survey & lay out tenn acres of land, by the direction of the sd Commissioners, but could not compleat the survey then for want of time.

+
1732
Novr: 22

On Wedensday ye 22d of Novr: 1732 Capt Robt North Mr Thomas Todd & Capt John Boreing three of the Commissioners for Jones's Town mett upon the above sd land called Cole's Harbour & order'd the Surveyor of Baltemore County to compleat the survey of the sd Town according to the meets & bounds agreed upon by the Commissioners at their first meeting which Courses shall be enter'd when returned to the Commissioners by the sd Surveyor. Some smal time afterwards the said Mr Philip Jones Surveyr compleated the Survey of the said town which was included in the following Courses & Distances according to the Certificate of the same by him return'd into Baltemore County Records. viz Jones's-Town Begining at a large Stone on the East side of Jones's Falls & runing thence for the Out bounds of the same, South 33° 30' East 30 perches. thence South 43° East 15 perches. thence North 49° East 4 perches. thence South East 20 pchs. thence South 49° West 4 perches. thence South East 2 perches. thence N 49° East 4 perches. thence South East 12 perches. thence South 17° East 21 perches. thence North 73° East 16 perches. thence

North 17° West 25 perches. thence North West
37 perches. thence South 49° West 4 perches.
thence North 43° West 14 perches. thence
North 33° 30′ West 28 perches. then by a
straight line to the begining stone containing
tenn Acres of land more or less.

No: 1:
+   July 20: 1733   Then Mr Jno: Gardner took up a
Lott in Jones's-town No: 1: and paid 2/6 the Clerk's
fee for entering the same & finish'd a house thereon
as order'd by Act of Assembly in the limited time.

No: 4:
+   July 20: 1733   Then Edward Fell, by his Attry in
Fact took up a Lott in Jones's town No: 4: and paid
the Clerks fee by his sd Attry for entering the same.

No: 6:
+   July 20: 1733   Then Mr Wm Fell took up a Lott
in Jones's-town No: 6: and paid the Clerk's fee for
entering the same.

No: 5:
+   July 20: 1733   Then Thomas Bond (by his Proxy)
took up a Lott in Jones's town No: 5: and paid the
Clerk his fee (by Wm Fell his sd Proxy) for entering
the same.

No: 2:
+   August 13: 1733   Then Capt: Robt North took up
a Lott in Jones's-town No: 2: & paid the Clerk's fee
for entering the same.

+
No: 3:
  August 18: 1733   Then Capt John Cromwell (by
his Proxy Mr Philip Jones junr) took up a Lott in
Jones's Town No: 3: and paid the Clerk's fee (by his
sd Proxy) for entering the same.

·+
No: 17:
  August 20: 1733   Then Capt John Boreing one
of the Comissrs: for Jones's town took up a Lott in
sd town No: 17: for himself and paid the Clerk's fee
for ·entering the same.

No. 18:
+
  On the same day viz. Augt: 20: 1733 Capt John
Boreing took up a Lott in Jones's town No: 18: for
his son John Boreing junr and paid the Clerk's fee
for entering the same.

No: 7:
+
+
  September: 2: 1733   Then Capt John Cockey one
of the Comissrs: for Jones's-town took up a Lott in
said town No: 7:

  February 15: 1734/5   Then Capt John Boreing
one of the Commissrs for Jones's Town having
neglected to build upon two Lotts in sd Town viz.

No: 17   No: 17: & 18 which he had taken up formerly viz on
18   the 20th day of August 1733 took up the said two
Lotts the second time according to the same intent,
& for ye same purpose as formerly & paid the Clerk's
fees for the same

+   February 19: 1734/5 Then came Capt John
Cockey who inform'd me that the heirs or Excrs of
Capt John Cromwell (who on the 18th day of August
No: 3   1733 took up a Lott in Jones's town No: 3) had not
built a house large enough to secure the said Lott according to ye Act of Assembly and desir'd to take up
the said Lott No: 3: in his Son William Cockey's
name & for his use & paid ye fee for ye same.

+   February 19: 1734/5 Then Capt John Cockey
having elaps'd the time of building a house on his
No: 7   Lott in Jones's town No: 7 desir'd the sd Lott No:
7 might be enter'd again in his own name & paid the
Clerk's fee for the same.

+   February 20: 1734/5 Then came Mr William
+   Fell & alcidged that there has been no house built
No: 4   upon the Lott No: 4: which he took up in the name
of his Brother Edward Fell on the 20th day of July
1733 by which neglect Edward Fell his right to the
sd Lott ceases and is lyable to be taken up a second
time which the sd William Fell now does in his own
name & for his own use & his heirs forever & paid
my fee

On the 20th day of Febr: 1734/5 Then Mr William
No: 15   Fell took up the four following Lotts in Jones's Town
16   viz: No: 15: 16: 19: 20: in his own name & for his
+ 19   own use & his heirs & he paid the Clerk's fees for
20   the same

March 5: 1734/5 Then Mr Wm Fell took up two
No: 8:   Lotts in Jones's town No: 8: & 9: and pay'd the
+ 9:   Clerk's fee for entering the same

May 10: 1735 Then Coll John Smith took up a
No: 14   Lott in Jones's Town No: 14. and paid the Clerk's
+   fee for entering the same.

November 8: 1735 Then Thomas Mathews took
No: 10   up the Lott No: 10 in Jones's Town & paid the Clerk's
+   fee for entering the same.

Augt: 14: 1736   Then Capt John Boreing having
No: 17   neglected building upon his Lott No: 17 according to
+   Law came and had the same reenter'd in his own
name and paid the Clerks fee for the same

+   Septr: 21: 1736   Then Mr William Fell having
neglected to build as the Law directs upon his Lotts
No: 15   No: 15: 16: & 19 he desir'd they might be taken up
16   the second time and enter'd in his own name & for
19   his own proper use & his heirs which accordingly is
now done.

Septr: 21: 1736   Then George Walker Clerk of
No: 20   Jones's town took up in sd Town the Lott No: 20
+   which was formerly viz on the 20th day of Febr:
1734/5 taken up by Mr William Fell but not secur'd
as the Law directs by building thereon.

+   Decr: 27: 1736   Mr Wm Fell having neglected to
build upon the two Lotts in Jones's Town (within the
No: 8:   time limited by Act of assembly) No: 8: & 9 for which
9:   he desires to have the said two Lotts No: 8 & 9 reentered in his own name & for his own use & his heirs

+   Decr 31: 1736   Then came Docr Buckler Partridge
No: 11:   and desir'd the Lott No: 11: in Jones's town might
be entered for himself & his heirs which accordingly
is now done

+   July 2: 1737   Then came Docr: Buckler Partridge
& represented that whereas Thomas Mathews having
neglected to comply with the requisites mentioned in
No: 10   the Act of Assembly his right to the Lott No: 10 in
Jones's-town falls & is rendered Null therefor the said
Partridge desires the sd Lott may be entered in his
own name which now is accordingly done

+   Augt: 30: 1737   Then came Mr Thomas Tayler
No. 12   of Baltemore Co'ty and took up the Lott No: 12 in
Jones's town & desir'd it might be register'd in his
name & for his use which is now accordingly done.

+   Augt: 30: 1737   Then George Walker took up in
his own name & for his own use & his heirs the Lott
No: 13   No: 13 in Jones's town & Register'd the same

March 20: 1737/8 Then Mr Wm Fell order'd the
No: 16 Lott No: 16 in Jones's Town which he had formerly
+ (viz on the 21: of September 1736) taken up to be
Register'd in his name & for his use which accordingly now is done

+ June 6th: 1738 Then George Walker Clerk of
Jones's Town (having neglected to build upon the
No: 20 Lott No: 20: according to Act of Assembly) desires
that the said Lott No: 20 may be Register'd in his
own name & accordingly it is this day done

+ June 20: 1738 Then George Walker sold all his
No: 13 Right Title & interest of in and to the Lott No: 13
in Jones's Town in Baltemore County unto Redman
Dearing and now it is Register'd in his own name &
for his own use

+ June 29: 1738 Then George Walker sold & trans-
ferr'd all his Right Title & interest of in and to the
No: 20 Lott No: 20 in Jones's town in Baltemore County
unto Joshua Hall and now it is Register'd in his own
name & for his own use.

+ July 18: 1738 Then Mr William Fell (having
neglected to build within eighteen months upon the
No: 9. Lott No: 9: in Jones's town since his last taking up
the same viz Decr: 27: 1736) he requests by his note
of hand the sd Lott No: 9: in said town might be
register'd in the name & for the use of John Boreing
& his heirs which accordingly is now done.

+ July 18: 1738 Then Mr William Fell (having
No: 8. neglected to build on the Lott No: 8: in Jones's town
within eighteen months after his last registring the
same desir'd the said Lott No: 8 might be reenter'd
in this Register in his own name & for his own use
which is now accordingly done.

+ Novr 29: 1739 John Connell representing to me
the Register of Jones's town in Baltemore County
No: 13 that whereas the Lott No: 13 in sd town was formerly
taken up viz on the 30 Augt: 1737 & by him trans-
ferr'd to Redman Dearing on the 20th of June 1738
but they having both neglected to build thereon within
the time limited by law he desires that the said Lott
may be enter'd in the Register of the sd town for his
own use which is now accordingly done

+   Aprile 7: 1740 Whereas Capt Robert North one of the Commissioners of Jones's Town in Baltemore County with others of the said Commissioners apprehends that all the Lotts in said town formerly taken up & not built upon in the time limited by act of Assembly now falls Vacant & lyable to be taken up anew for the use & benefite of the sd Town the sd

No: 8: Capt Robt North desires that the Lotts No: 8: 9: 16
9: in the sd town may be entered in his own name & for
16: his own use—which is accordingly now done

+   Aprile 8th 1740 Then came Mrs Mary Hanson
No: 5: and desir'd the Lotts No: 5: 6: in Jones's Town in
6: Baltemore County may be enter'd in her name & for her use one of which Lotts is not sufficiently cover'd by building according to the Act of Assembly and paid the Clerks fees for the same

+   Aprile 8th 1740 Three of the Commissioners for erecting a Town in Baltemore County called (by Act of Assembly) Jones's town mett in the sd Town with George Walker their Clerk and order'd their sd Clerk to enter in his Register of the sd Town any Lotts that may or shall be found vacant according to the Act of Assembly to be further taken up by any person whatsoever who shall pay or secure to the Commissioners of the sd town the sume of one hundred & fifty pounds of Tob: for each Lott to be applied to the use of the sd Town with the accustomary Clerks fees

The Commissioners who mett as above sd were

Capt   ⎧ THOMAS SHEREDINE   ⎫
      ⎨ JOHN BOREING   ⎬ GEO: WALKER
      ⎩ ROBT NORTH   ⎭ Clk:

+   Aprile 8th 1740 Then came Mr Alexander Lawson & desired George Walker Clerk of Jones's Town in Baltemore County to enter in his Register for the

No: 12: sd town in his name & for his use the Lott No: 12 of the sd Town which is now accordingly done

Aprile 8: 1740 Then Capt Thomas Sheredine one of the Commissioners of Jones's Town orderd George Walker Clk: to ye sd Comissrs to enter in his Register

No: 11: the Lott No: 11: in his name & for his use which is
+   now accordingly done.

+   Aprile 8: 1740 Then Mr Edward Fell desir'd
George Walker Clk: of Jones's town in Baltemore
Co'ty to enter in his own name & for his own use the
No: 20   Lott No: 20: in the sd Town which was formerly
taken up on the 20th day of Febr: 1734/5 by Mr Wm:
Fell then again taken up by George Walker on the
21st of Septr 1736 then reenter'd in the sd Walker
his name on the 6th day of June 1738 which sd
Walker afterwards sold his right & title in & to the sd
Lott No: 20: unto Joshua Hall on the 29th of June
1738 which sd Lott No: 20: is now enter'd in the
name & for the use of the sd Edward Fell who paid
the Clk: his fee for the same.

      Augt 18: 1740 Then came Mr William Fell and
being apprehensive that his claime and Title to the
No: :   Lott No: 4: in Jones's town fell & ceased for want of
building a house upon it according to Act of Assembly
which Lott he formerly took up on the 20th day of
Febr: 1734/5 and desired that the said Lott No: 4
may be again entered in his name which now is ac·
cordingly done.

      Novr: 19: 1741 Then came Mr Alexander Law-
son & desired George Walker Clerk of Jones's Town
in Baltemore County to reenter the two Lotts in the
No: 11 :   said town No: 11: 12: in his own name & for his own
12 :   use which now is accordingly done & he promises &
obliges himself to satisfie any person whose right it
shall prove to be to receive the purchase money or
tobacco for the same.

By an Act of Assembly made at a session held at the City of
Annapolis the fifth Day of August Seventeen Hundred & forty
five the Towns heretofore called Baltimore Town and Jones
Town were incorporated into one Town by the Name of Baltimore Town, and the Lotts hereafter entered on either side of
the Bridge to be known and distinguished by the Name of
Lotts in Baltimore Town.

MARCH the 8th 1745/6

Then met Colo. William Hammond Captn. Robert North Doctor Geo Buchanan Captn Darby Lux and Mr. William Fell five of the Comrs. for Baltimore Town who proceeded to make Choice of Charles Crooke For their Clk. who was accordingly Qualify'd for that purpose, by Doctor Geo. Buchanan a Magistrate for Baltimore County and also four of the Comrs. agreed with Mr William Fell, to dig holes for and sett in as many locust posts, of three & ahalf feet long & four inches square as Shall be necessary for the said Town at fifteen pence p post the said posts to be sett at lease two feet in the Ground. Colo. William Hammond one of the said Comrs. is also appointed to collect & receive all Debts and arrearages due to the aforesaid Town and likewise that what part of the said arrearages shall be come due in Tobo. The said Hammond is impowered to discount with the several persons from whom the same is or shall become Due at the rate of Ten shillgs p Cent.

It is likewise ordered that the Clerk give Mr. Thomas Franklin Notice in writing to meet the Comrs. on the seventeenth instant, in Order to agree for resurveying the Town & making a plan thereof—

MONDAY MARCH 16th 1746

The following Gentlemen Comrs of Baltimore Town Viz

MAJR THOMAS SHEREDINE
DR. GEO BUCHANAN
COL. WILLIAM HAMMOND
CAPN. ROBERT NORTH
CAPTN DARBY LUX

Mett at Mr. Edward Dagans in the said Town and proceeded to business and understanding that Mr. Charles Crook is very ill and uncapable of attending the business of their Clk. Unanimously agree To displace him the said Charles Crook, and Have Chose William Lux their Clk. in his room and he was Sworn in the sd. Office Accordingly

They also chose Mr. Alexander Lawson Comr of the said Town in the room of Mr. William Fell deceased.

The commissioners also gave Mr. William Rogers an Order on Mrss Jane Bourdllion for £12 due on approv'd acco,t against the reverend Mr. Benedict Bourdillion for takeing up lotts in

Baltimore Town also gave an Order on Colo. William Hammond to Mr William Rogers for £12 out of the money he has in his hands.

They also agree that William Lux should receive the Debts due to the Commissioners for Fallen lotts.

They also agreed with Captain Robert North to fence in part of the Town Over the falls formerly called Jones's Town in such manner as he shall think proper for which he is to have at the rate of £8 p thousand for Oak Railes and £3 p thousand for the stakes and to set up the same and be compleated by the last of April.

They also agreed with Colo. William Hammond to Set up three Gates, two of ten feet wide in the clear within the posts an I One of five feet wide in the Clear within the posts White O: k framed and locust posts and Sils.

FRIDAY 24th JULY 1747

The Commissioners met and were present Viz.

> Dr. Geo Buchanan
> Colo. William Hamond
> Capn. Rort. North
> Capn. Darby Lux
> Mr. Thomas Harrison

The Commissioners examining what money is due to Balto. Town for retaking up fallen lotts do find that there is 25 lotts which the proprietors have not paid for according to the following list at forty shillings p lott Viz.

BALTIMORE TOWN

Colo. William Hammond	1 Lott No 46
Dr. Geo. Walker	7 Do 53, 10, 14, 42, 43, 44, 39
Mr. Edward Fottril	4 Do 11, 40, 41, 39
Mr. John Humphreys	1 Do 42
Mr. Joseph Hooper	2 Do 44, 44
Joshua Hall	1 Do 10
Mr. William Rogers	3 Do 14, 42, 42
Revd. Benedict Bourdillion	6 Do 26, 35, 40, 41, 26, 35

JONES'S TOWN 24 lotts viz.

Dr. Geo. Walker	2 lotts	No.	20, 20
Captn. John Boring	3 lotts	"	17, 18, 17
Captn. John Cockey	2 lotts	"	3, 7
Mr. William Fell	9 lotts	"	4, 15, 16, 19, 8, 9, 10, 9, 8
Dr. Buckler Patridge	1 lott	"	10
Mr. Alexander Lawson	1 lott	"	12
Mr. John Connell	1 lott	"	13
Miss Mary Hanson	2 lotts	"	5, 6
Captn. Robert North	3 lotts	"	8, 9, 16

At 150 lb Tobo. each lott & have Ordered their Clerk to raise
accots for the Same and Charge propriators Debtor therewith
and when he receives the money to Carry it to the Credit of the
sd. Town, by Keeping an acct. in his book of General Charges
for the said Town. They also Ordered their Clk. to give Mr.
Thomas Franklin notice to meet the Comrs. on the Second Monday in September next in Order to resurvey the Town also Ordered the Clerk to put up publick notes for any person to agree
for Eighty locust posts to be three feet & half long & to square
four inches for bounds for the lotts & that Darby Lux and
Thomas Harrison are impowered to agree and Contract for the
same   They also Ordered the Clerk to transcribe the Record
book of Baltimore and Jones's Town into another proper book
& agree to allow him for the Same.

MONDAY August 10th 1747

The Commissioners met and were present

Majr. Thomas Sheredine	Capt. Darby Lux
Dr. Geo. Buchanan	Mr. Alexander Lawson
Colo. William Hammond	Mr Thomas Harrison
Capt. Robt. North	

Captain Robert North brought in his acct. for Fencing in
part of the Town Over the falls Formerly Called Jones's
Town Which passed the Commissioners and Ordered the
Clerk to give him Credit accordingly.

SEPTEMBER 16th 1747

Came Dr. Geo. Buchanan, Colo. William Hammond, Capt. Darby Lux and Mr. Thomas Harrison
No. 26   desiring that the lott in Baltimore Town No. 26 first
taken up by James Powel On 15th January 1729/30
afterwards by the reverend Mr. Benedict Bourdillion
twice first on the 15th May 1741 and then on March

4th 1742/3 now being forfeited for riot building thereon according to act of assembly desire it may be enter'd in their names Each an Equal Share, also the

No. 21 lott No 21 taken up the Sixteenth of September 1734 by the Rever'd Mr. Joseph Hooper, likewise the lott

22 No. 22 Taken up the 28th June 1734 by the Revd. Mr. Joseph Hooper which two lotts being forfeited by neglecting to build thereon according to act of Assembly. They also Desire that the said two lotts may be also enterd in their names each an equal share.

Also the Lott 39 taken up first by John Giles on the

No. 39 fifth day of November 1731 afterwards by Thomas Woodward On the Eight of August 1734 afterwards by Edward Fotterill on the 24th of September 1741 which lott being forfeited for not building thereon according to act of Assembly desire may be entered in their Names Each on Equal Share————————

SEPTEMBER 18th. 1747

Whereas an act of assembly empowering any Person to make Land below the Banks of Baltimore Town and where the water usually flows giving the improver thereof a fee simple therein and in pursuance to which William Hammond has applied to me William Lux Clerk of the said Town to enter for him the said Hammond as follows Viz.

beginning at the South corner of a Lott No. 48 belonging to a Mr. William Savory and runing thence three Perches, then West the breadth of said Lott, then to the West Corner of the said Lott then with the said Lott, to the aforesaid Begining the said Hammond setting forth that his Intention is to Make a wharf and Build thereon according to the act aforesaid—

Mr. Alexander Lawson applied also to enter his Preemption of making out Ground into the water the Extent of My Lott and as far out as conveniently he can.

Also Captain Darby Lux desires me the said Clerk to enter his Preemption of making out Ground into the Water the extent of his Lott and as far out as conveniently he can

SATURDAY SEPTEMBER 26. 1747—

Mr. Joseph Taylor came and representing to me William Lux clerk of Baltimore Town that the Lott No. 5. in the said Town in that Part formerly Jones's Town formerly taken up by Thomas Bond on July 20th. 1733. afterwards by Mary Hanson on April 8th. 1740 is become vacant by Not building thereon according to act of Assembly and desires the said Lott may be enter'd in the Name of Edward Fell son of William—And also the Lott Number 6. in Jones's Town taken up by William Fell on July 20th. 1733 afterwards by Mary Hanson on April 8th. 1740 is also become forfeited by Not building thereon according to act of Assembly, requests me the said Clerk to Enter the Same in the name of Ann Fell which is now accordingly done—he having paid thirty shillings in Lieu of Three hundred Pounds of Tobacco for the same.

No. 5 appears in the left margin beside the line beginning "No. 5."
No. 6 appears in the left margin beside the line beginning "William—And also".

NOVEMBER 19th, 1747.

Whereas by act of Assembly passed at a Session held at annapolis July 8th. 1747 the Land lying between Baltimore Town and Jones's Town was ordered to be laid out into Lotts pursuant to which Order the Commissioners this day met and employed Nicholas Ruxton Gay to Survey the Same and lay it out into Lotts with convenient Streets and alleys which he accordingly did in the Presence of the Major Part of the Commissioners and by their directions as by a Certificate and platt hereunto annexed appears begining at the Lott Number Sixty One and ending at the Lott Number One hundred and fiften for the Property of Thomas Harrison begining at the Lott Number One hundred and Sixteen and Ending at Number One Hundred and eighteen the Property of Thomas Sligh & Thomas Sheredine Begining at Number One hundred and Nineteen, the Property of Alexander Lawson and Ending at Number One hundred and forty four—

SATURDAY, JANUARY 28th. 1748.

The Commissioners met and were present

MAJOR THOMAS SHEREDINE

COL'O. WILLIAM HAMMOND

CAPT. ROBERT NORTH

CAPT. DARBY LUX

Ordered that the Clerk set public Notes up that every Inhabitant of any House in Town wherein there is a Chimney in use, do provide themselves with a Ladder to reach the Top of the Roof of the House by the Last of March next Under the Penalties of the said act. also if any Chimney is found blazing out at the Top under the like Penalties. They also order the Clerk to apply to those persons who are indebted to the Commissioners for taking up lotts in the said Town and have their final answers..

The Commissioners agree to Meet on the first Monday of every Month at Mr. William Rogers at 2 oClock in the afternoon—

SATURDAY JANUARY 28th, 1748.

Captain Robert North came and representing to me William Lux clerk of Baltimore that the Lott No. 7 No. 7 in the said Town in that part formerly Jones's Town formerly taken up September 2nd 1733 by Captain John Cockey afterwards on february 19th 1734/5 by the said Captain John Cockey is become Vacant by not building thereon according to act of Assembly and desires the said lott may be entered in his Name which is Now accordingly done: Also No. 8 Lott No. 8 in Jones's Town formerly taken up March 5th 1734/5 by Mr. William Fell also on December 27th 1736 by the said William Fell and on July 18th. 1738. by the said William Fell and on April 7th. 1740. by Captain Robert North is also become Vacant and liable to be taken up by not building thereon according to the said Act of Assembly desires that the said Lott may be entered in his Name which is Now accordingly done he having paid the Clerk's fees for entering the same and thirty shillings the Purchase Money thereof.

MONDAY FEBRUARY 6th 1748

The Commissioners met and were present

MAJOR THOMAS SHEREDINE   COLO. WILLIAM HAMMOND
CAPTAIN ROBERT NORTH   CAPTAIN DARBY LUX

Ordered that when any Person applies to the Clerk to take up any Lott either in Baltimore or in Jones's Town that they pay down the Money to the Clerk, or the Clerk is not to enter it and when it is in Tobacco to receive it at 12/6 p Ct or a Note payable to the Commissioners on Demand.

WEDNESDAY MARCH 15th 1748

Came Captain Darby Lux in behalf of himself Doctor George Buchanan, Colonel William Hammond and Mr. Thomas Harrison and representing to me William Lux Clerk of Baltimore Town, that the three No. 21 Lotts in Baltimore Town No. 21, 22 and 26 formerly 22 taken up by them on September 16th 1747 are not 26 built upon in the Time limited by act of Assembly and desires that the said three Lotts may be again enter'd in their Names each an equal share, having paid six pounds for taking them up and the Clerk's fees for the same, which is now accordingly done—

SATURADY MARCH 25th. 1749.

Came Mary Woodward and representing to me William Lux clerk of Baltimore Town that the lott in No. 39 Baltimore Town No 39. taken up September 16th. 1748 by Messrs George Buchanan, Colo. William Hammond and Captain Darby Lux, and Mr. Thomas Harrison is become Vacant by their not building thereon in the Time Limited by act of Assembly and desires that the said Lott may be entered in the Name of her Son John Woodward which is now accordingly done. She having paid two Pounds for taking it up and the Clerks fees for the same — — —

MONDAY MAY 1st 1749

The Commissioners met and were present

MAJOR THOMAS SHEREDINE   DR. GEORGE BUCHANAN
COLO WILLIAM HAMMOND   CAPTAIN DARBY LUX

They chose Mr. William Rogers a Commissioner of Baltimore Town in the Room of Capt. Robert North deceased —

SATURDAY JUNE 10th. 1749.

Came Mr. Thomas Sligh and representing to me William Lux clerk of Baltimore Town that the two No. 11 lotts in Jones's Town No. 11 & 12 formerly taken up 12 by Mr. Alexander Lawson Viz November 19th. 1741. is become Vacant by not building thereon according to act of Assembly and desires that the said Two lotts may be entered in his Own Name and for his own use which is now accordingly done he having pass'd his Note to the Commissioners of Baltimore Town for Three Hundred pounds of Good, sound clean Merchantable Tobacco or the same to be paid in Cash at Twelve Shillings and Six pence pr Hundred.

JUNE 15th 1750

Whereas by act of Assembly passed at a Session held at Annapolis in May 1750—the quantity of twenty five acres of land adjoining to that part of Baltimore Town formerly Jones's Town was ordered to be laid out into Lotts agreeable to which the Commissioners this day met and Order'd Nicholas Ruxton Gay to survey the same & lay it out into Lotts which he accordingly did as by a certificate and platt thereof hereunto annex'd appears begining at Number Twenty One Ending at the Lott Number Seventy one the property of Thomas Sheredine and Thomas Sligh

THURSDAY AUGUST 30th. 1750—

The Commissioners met and were present.

MAJOR THOMAS SHEREDINE	MR THOMAS HARRISON
CAPTAIN DARBY LUX	MR. ALEXANDER LAWSON
MR WILLIAM ROGERS	

The Commissioners chose unanimously Mr Brean Philpot Junr. a commissioner of Baltimore Town in the Room of Dr George Buchanan—deceased of which the Clerk is to give him Notice. The Commissioners agree to meet on Monday the 10th. September Next at 9 oClock in the morning at the House of Mr. William Rogers and ordered the Clerk to give Mr. Philpot. Notice thereof which he according did the succeeding day—

MONDAY SEPTEMBER 10th 1750—

The Commissioners met and were present—

MAJOR THOMAS SHEREDINE   MR. ALEXANDER LAWSON
CAPTAIN DARBY LUX   MR. WILLIAM ROGERS
MR THOMAS HARRISON   MR. BRIAN PHILPOT JUR
COLO. WILLIAM HAMMOND

Colo. William Hammond brought in his account which the Commissioners allowed and Ordered him to have credit for. Captain Darby Lux brought in his account brought for a Book to enter the Proceedings of the Town in which was allowed and the Clerk order'd to pay him the Balance. Mr. William Rogers brought in his account for fencing in the town which was allow'd and Ordered to give credit for. also his account for Making up the fence of the Town and putting up locust posts at the End of each lott which was allowed and Order'd to give him Credit for—

The Commissioners taking into Consideration the detriment that accrues to this Town by Sundry persons taking up Lotts therein and Neglecting to pay the Purchase Money to remove which they order that when any Person applys to the Clerk to enter any Lott on the South Side of the Bridge that he doth not enter it unless they pay down the Purchase Money and fees thereon; and for any Lott on the North Side of the bridge that he doth not enter any unless they pay down the inspector's Notes or the Money for the Same—at the prices Tobacco then bears, which price is left to the discretion of the Clerk— The Commissioners Order the Clerk to apply to Mr. William Chapman and Major Charles Ridgely to know if either of them will pay the Debt due from Mr. Edward Fotterel of 8£ and if both refuse to pay that then the Clerk apply to Daniel Dulany Junr. Esquire to issue a Writ in Anne Arundel County court against Mr. William Chapman as administrator of Mr. Edward Fotterell for the Same— The Commissioners resolved to Levey a Tax of one Shilling Currency pr. Annum on Each lott in the Town towards defraying the wages of the Clerk and that the same be levied for Years *past* ending March 25th 1749. Also One Shilling Currency on Each lott for a locust Post which is set up at the end of Each lott and Order'd The Clerk to make out accounts against the Several Proprietors of the lotts and demand them and return a list of what he receives to the Com-

missioners at their next meeting. The Commissioners order
the Clerk to transcribe in a Seperate folio book all the Laws
relating to this Towns from the original Law down, and also
to procure all the Laws relating to Towns for their Perusal.
The Commissioners order the Clerk to put up advertisements
to inform all Persons that they have order'd the Town fence
to be made up, and that they have employed John Walker
to keep up the same and if any Person suffers their Hogs
sheep or Geese to trespass on the Inhabitants as they have
hitherto done, that they will immediately Order them to
be destroyed— The Commissioners taking into consideration that three Lotts taken up by Dr George Buchanan,
Colo. William Hammond Capt. Darby Lux and Mr Thomas
Harrison on the 16th. September 1747. and also by Captain Darby Lux in behalf of himself, Dr George Buchanan,
Colo. William Hammond and Mr Thomas Harrison on March
15. 1748 have been twice taken and not built upon according to act of Assembly and that it impedes the increase of
the Town by having these Lotts unbuilt upon Viz. No. 21. 22.
26. the Commissioners have therefore resolved to put the same
Lotts up to public Vendue on Saturday the sixth day of October
Next also the Materials of the Brick House standing opposite
to Daniel Barsuets in the Street which is to be pull'd down as
a Nuisance order'd that the Clerk put up advertisements at ye
most public places

The Commissioners agree to John Walker to keep up the
Town fence for which they are to allow him forty Shillings
Currency pr. Annum his time to commence from September
29th. 1750 The Commissioners order'd the Clerk to pay Mr.
Alexander Lawson the Balance of Captain Robert North's
account; and what Money he has in his hands over and above
the payments before Order'd with what he may receive to
pay to Mr. William Rogers they also ordered to give Colo.
William Hammond and Captain Darby Lux credit for an
Overcharge in their subscription for making good the Town
fence, Ten Shillings Each they also order'd their Clerk to
apply to all those Persons indebted to the town and collect their
respective Debts and if they refuse to pay, then to issue warrants.

The Commissioners agree to meet at Mr. William Rogers
on Saturday the Sixth day of October Next at 9 oClock in the
Morning—

SATURDAY SEPTEMBER 15th 1750

The Came Messrs. Darby Lux Mr Thomas Harrison and Colo. William Hammond and representing to me William Lux clerk of Baltimore Town that the three lotts in Baltimore Town formerly taken up by Doctor George Buchanan Colo. William Hammond Captain Darby Lux and Mr. Thomas Harrison on the 16th. September 1747 afterwards by Captain Darby Lux in behalf of himself and them, on 15th. March 1748. Viz

No. 21   21. 22. 26 are again become Vacant by not being built
22   on in the Time prescribed by act of Assembly. and de-
26   sires that the said 3 Lotts No. 21. 22. 26 may be en-
ter'd in their Names Each an Equal Share, which is Now Done, they having paid Six Pounds Currency for the Purchase Money, and the fees thereof.

SATURDAY OCT 6. 1750—

The Commissioners met and were present

MR THOMAS HARRISON   MR ALEXANDER LAWSON
MR WILLIAM ROGERS   MR BRIAN PHILPOT JUNR.

The Commissioners Order'd the Clerk apply to Major Charles Ridgely for the Debt due from Mr. Edward Fotterell of 8£ Mr. Alexander Lawson having applied to Mr. William Chapman who declared that he had delivered up the Houses and Lotts to Major Charles Ridgely who must pay the said Debts: The Commissioners Order'd the Clerk to apply to Charles Carroll Esquire for his lease to set the fence of the town on his land and obtain his Answer in Writing against their Next Meeting: The Commissioners order'd the Clerk to apply to Mr John Ridgely to finish the Causeway of the Bridge according to agreement

The Commissioners taking into consideration the Sale of three lotts No. 21. 22. 26. which were to be sold this day by Public Vendue do resolve that to prevent the said Lotts from Selling at an Under Price that they will bid to the following Prices—Viz for the Lott No. 26. Sixty Pounds Currency for the Lott No. 22 Sixty Pounds Currency and for the Lott No. 21. fifty Pounds Currency and order'd the Clerk to bid to those Prices in their Behalf and agreed the following to be the Conditions of Sale the Purchaser to pay down the Money in three Months on which the Commissioners will order the Lott or

Lotts to be entered in his Name, or if the Purchaser shall want to have immediate Possession on giving good Security for the Money to the Satisfaction of the Commissioners, the Commissioners will Order the Lott to be entered in his Name immediately the purchaser to build on the Lott within the space of Eighteen Months from the 10th day of September 1750 a House that shall Cover at least four hundred feet of ground according to the Directions of the act of Assembly—

The Commissioners appoint Nicholas Rogers Junr. Auctioneer for which he is to be allowed five Shillings Currency for Selling Each Lott and five Shillings for the House— The Commissioners adjourn'd themselves to three oClock in the Evening— At the appointed Time the Commissioners met and were present—

COLO. WILLIAM HAMMOND
MR. ALEXANDER LAWSON
MR. WILLIAM ROGERS
MR. BRIAN PHILPOT JUNR.

when the lotts were set up and sold as follows Viz.

Number Twenty Six to Mr. Alexander Lawson for Sixty Pounds Currency

Number Twenty One to Mr. Brian Philpot Junr. for fifty three Pounds Currency

Number Twenty Two to Mr. William Lux in behalf of the Commissioners for fifty Seven Pounds, The Material of the Brick House to Mr. Alexander Lawson for Thirty Pounds Current Money.

WEDNESDAY November 22. 1750—

Then came Mr. William Cockey and representing to me William Lux clerk of Baltimore Town that the Two Lotts in the said Town in that Part which No. 7 was formerly Jones Town No 7 & 8 lastly taken up 8 by Captain Robert North on Saturday January 28th 17.18 are become Vacant by not building thereon according to Act of Assembly and desires the Two Lotts aforesaid No 7 & 8 may be entered in his Name and for his use which is now accordingly done he having paid Two Pounds Eleven Shillings Currency for the Purchase Money thereof and the Clerks fees for the same——

March 2nd. 1750 Mrs. Sarah Bowring came and
entered the Lott in Baltimore town on the North East
No. 28   side of the Bridge No 28. purchased by her from
Messrs. Thomas Sheredine, and Thomas Sligh the
proprietors as by Certificate produced to me March
2nd. 1750   Mr. Moses Rutter came and entered the
Lott in Baltimore Town on the North East side of the
No. 29   Bridge No 29. purchased by him from Messrs. Thomas
Sheredine and Thomas Sligh the proprietors as by
Certificate produced to me — —

March 30th. 1751. Doctor Henry Cumming came
and entered the Lott in Baltimore Town on the North
No. 61   East Side of the Bridge No. 61. purchased by him
from Messrs. Thomas Sheredine, and Thomas Sligh
the proprietors as by Certificate produced to me.

April 12th, 1751. came Major Thomas Sheredine
and Mr Thomas Sligh and representing that the Two
Lotts in Baltimore Town in that Part formerly Jones's
No. 11   Town No. 11 & 12 last taken up by Mr. Thomas
12   Sligh on June 10th. 1749 are become Vacant by not
building thereon in the Time prescribed by act of assembly and desires the said Two Lotts might be entered in their Names they having paid two pounds
Eleven Shillings in Lieu of 300 lb. Tobacco for taking
up the same.

No. 43   April 29th. 1751. Mr. Brian Philpot Junr. took up
44, 45   the Eleven lotts on the North East side of the
46, 47   Bridge No. 43. 44. 45. 46. 47. 49. 50. 51. 52. 53.
49, 50   54 purchased by him from Messrs. Thomas Shere-
51, 52   dine and Thomas Sligh the proprietors thereof as by
53, 54   certificate produced to me ——

May 3rd. 1751. Mr. Edmund Talbott came and
entered the Lott in Baltimore Town on the North
No. 55   East side of the Bridge No 55 purchased by him
from Messrs. Thomas Sheredine and Thomas Sligh
as by Certificate produced—

May 15. 1751. Mr. John Ensor Junr. came and
entered the Lott in Baltimore Town on the North
No. 24   East side of the Bridge No 24. together with the
square Piece of Ground adjoining the Begining of the
Town and containing by Estimation about half an

acre or a quarter of an Acre purchased by him from Thomas Sheredine and Thomas Sligh the proprietors as by Certificate produced to me — —

June 15. 1751. Mr. Abraham Towson came and entered the lott in Baltimore Town on the North East No 70 Side of the Bridge No. 70 purchased by him from Thomas Sheredine and Thomas Sligh the proprietors as by Certificate produced to me— — —

June 15. 1751 Mr. William Towson enter'd the Lotts in Baltimore Town on the North East Side of No. 48 the Bridge No 48 and 66 purchased by him from 66 Thomas Sheredine & Thomas Sligh the proprietors as by Certificate produced to me—

June 17. 1751. Mr. Laurence Watson came and en- No. 35 ter'd the Lott in Baltimore Town No 35 purchased by him from Thomas Sheredine and Thomas Sligh as by Certificate produced to me—

June 21. 1751. Mrs. Sarah Boring came and en- ter'd the Two Lotts in Baltimore Town in the North No 26 East Part No 26. and 27 purchased by her from the 27 Proprietors Thomas Sheredine and Thomas Sligh as by Certificate produced to me—

July 1st. 1751. Christopher Strangwigs came and entered the Lott in Baltimore Town in the North No. 59 East Part No 59. purchased by him from the Pro- prietors Thomas Sheredine and Thomas Sligh as by Certificate produced to me—

July 1st. 1751. Samuel Hook came and entered the No 86 Lott in Baltimore Town No 86 purchased by him from the Proprietor Thomas Harrison together with a part of the Lot Number Sixty One containing thirty two feet front at the west End and adjoining the Lott No 56.

July 1st. 1751. George Michael Hartman came and No. 87 entered the Lott in Baltimore Town Number Eighty Seven purchased by him from the Proprietor Thomas Harrison together with a Part of the Lott No. Sixty One containing Thirty two feet front of the West part adjoining the Part Samuel Hook Bought — —

July 4th. 1751 George Picket entered the Lott in Baltimore Town in the North East side of the Bridge

No. 34   No 34 purchased by him from the Proprietors Thomas Sheredine and Thomas Sligh as by certificate produced to me — —

November 4. 1751. Moses Rutter entered the Lott in Baltimore Town on the East Side of the Bridge

No. 38   No. 38 purchased by him from the Proprietors Thomas Sheredine and Thomas Sligh as by a certificate produced to me — —

December 17. 1751. Patrick Gray entered the Lott in Baltimore Town on the North East side of the

No 58   Bridge No 58 purchased by him from the Proprietors Thomas Sheredine and Thomas Sligh as by certificate produced to me.——

December 15th. 1751. John Moor entered the Lott in Baltimore Town on the North East Side of the

No. 65   Bridge No 65. purchased by him from the Proprietors Thomas Sheredine and Thomas Sligh as by certificate produced to me —

December 19th. 1751. Hannah Hughes entered the Lotts in Baltimore Town on the North East Side of

No. 21   the Bridge No. 21. 71. purchased by her from the

71   Proprietors Thomas Sheredine and Thomas Sligh as by certificate produced to me—

January 2nd. 1752. Patrick G. Settleman entered the Lott in Baltimore Town on the North East side

No 57   of the Bridge No 57. purchased by him from the Proprietors Thomas Sheredine and Thomas Sligh as by certificate Produced to me— —

January 29th. 1752 William Nicolson came and entered the Lott in Baltimore Town on the North

No. 42   East side of the Bridge No 42 purchased by him from the Proprietors Thomas Sheredine and Thomas Sligh as by certificate produced to me

February 14. 1752 Came John Shepherd and entered the three lotts in Baltimore Town on the North

No. 39   East side of the Bridge No. 39. 40. 41 purchased by

40 41   him from the Proprietors Thomas Sheredine and Thomas Sligh as by certificate produced to me— —

FRIDAY JANUARY 25. 1750—

The commissioners met and were present
> MAJOR THOMAS SHEREDINE
> COLO. WILLIAM HAMMOND
> MR. THOMAS HARRISON
> MR. ALEXANDER LAWSON
> MR. WILLIAM LUX
> MR. BRIAN PHILPOT JUNR.

The Commissioners unanimously Chose Doctor William Lyon a Commissioner of Baltimore Town in the Room of Captain Darby Lux deceased and Order the Clerk to give him Notice accordingly: The Clerk having produced Mr. John Ridgely's Letter relating to the Causway of the Bridge, the Commissioners Ordered it to be read and afterwards filed for their further consideration at their next meeting: If any Person shoud apply to enter any Lott, or Lotts in the New addition of Baltimore Town belonging to Messrs. Thomas Sheredine & Thomas Sligh the Commissioners Order the Clerk to take a Minute of the Same on a Paper kept for that purpose in Order to enter them after the return of Mr Thomas Harrison Plott and certificate of the Lotts added to Baltimore by him: The Commissioners agree to meet on the fourth day of February next

MONDAY FEBRUARY 4th. 1750

The Commissioners met according to appointment but there not being at Majority they coud not proceed to Business — —

WEDNESDAY FEBRUARY 6. 1750—

The Commissioners met and were present.
> COLO. WILLIAM HAMMOND
> MR. THOMAS HARRISON
> MR ALEXANDER LAWSON
> MR. WILLIAM ROGERS

They Order the Clerk to apply to Mr. John Ridgely to finish the Causway of the Bridge compleatly it never having been finished according to agreement— The Clerk having laid before the Commissioners a Letter received from Charles Carroll Esqr. permitting him to put the Town fence on his land adjoining the said Town—It was read and the Clerk Order'd to return a

Letter of thanks in Answer thereto— The Commissioners Order the Clerk to put up advertisements for the Inhabitants of the Town to provide themselves with ladders before the Twenty fifth of March next and also to mention in the said advertisements that as Some Persons have willfully destroyed the Boundaries of some of the lotts in the said Town the Commissioners will give a Reward of Twenty Shilling to any Person who shall discover the offender or offenders. The Commissioners Order the Clerk to put up advertisements one Month before the fairs kept in the Town to inform all persons that they are not to erect any Booths or Sell any Liquor at the said fairs before they obtain License from the Clerk and pay him for the Same. The Clerk not to receive a Sum exceeding fifteen Shillings for any One Booth nor Less than Two Shillings and Six Pence to be applied to the use of ye Town.

WEDNESDAY, MARCH 28th 1751. /21

The Commissioners met and were present

CoLO. WILLIAM HAMMOND

MR. THOMAS HARRISON

MR. ALEXANDER LAWSON

MR. WILLIAM ROGERS

The Commissioners taking into consideration that Several of the Inhabitants of this Town have not supplied themselves with Ladders within the Time appointed at their Last Meeting Viz. the Twenty fifth of March and considering that several of those live in rented Houses and may Imagine that their Landlords are obliged to find such ladders have therefore thought proper to allow them untill the fifth day of April Next and order'd the Clerk to put up advertisements accordingly— And whereas several Persons permit stinking fish, dead creatures or carron to lie on their Lotts or in the Streets near their Doors which are very offensive Nusances and contrary to act of Assembly the Commissioners therefore Order the Clerk to put up advertisements to inform such Persons that they are to remove them also to command those inhabitants who keep Hogs in the Town to confine them within their Own inclosures before the first of April.

MONDAY MARCH 9th. 1752. 1.

The commissioners met and were present

MR. THOMAS HARRISON
MR. ALEXANDER LAWSON
MR. BRIAN PHILPOT JUNR. }Commissioners.
DOCTOR WILLIAM LYON
MR. WILLIAM ROGERS

The commissioners order the clerk to apply to Major Charles Ridgely for the debt of and due from Mr. Edward Fottrell and to obtain his answer in writing to lay before them at their Next Meeting—also to write to Mr John Ridgely to comply with his agreement in finishing the Causway of the Bridge and obtain his final answer against their Next Meeting. Mr. William Rogers Mr. Brian Philpot Junior and Doctor William Lyon are appointed to inspect the Boundaries of the Lotts and the Ladders to each chimney (according to act of Assembly annually) and to return an account of what are wanting at the next Meeting of the Commissioners—and also to cause all Nusances to be removed. Whereas many Rails which fenced in the Town have been taken away and destroyed, the Commissioners do therefore Order the Clerk to make inquiry whether any Person can inform them who is the offender and can prove it on them particularly the Reverend Thomas Chase, Doctor John Stevenson, Mr. William Payne or Sarah Walker the Commissioners having heard they were seen to take them away— The Commissioners Order the Clerk to apply to those indebted to the Town and if they do not immediately pay, then to issue Warrants also to Levey One Shilling pr Lott, ending 25th March 1752 and to collect it——

TUESDAY NOVEMBER 21st. 1752. 2

The Commissioners met and were Present

MR THOMAS HARRISON   MR WILLIAM ROGERS
MR ALEXANDER LAWSON   DOCTOR WILLIAM LYON

As many of the Rails which fenced in the Town have been taken away and destroyed it rendered the Remainder useless. The Commissioners therefore disposed of them to Mr Nicholas Rogers at the rate of five Pounds ten Shillings currency Pr Thousand and Order'd the Clerk to deliver them the next

Morning; Order'd a writ to be brought aginst William Payne for Burning the Town Rails and that Mr. Lloyd Buchanan be employed as Attorney— Order'd to inquire whether Proof cou'd be made of any Other Person burning or removing any of the Rails and commence Suits against them November 22nd. 1752. In obedience to the above Order I this day delivered Mr. Nicholas Rogers One Thousand Rails, and to Mr. Thomas Harrison twelve Hundred. I also made application to Mr. Lloyd Buchanan to issue a Writ against Mr Payne, but he was of opinion the Commissioners had No power to bring such action therefor cou'd not recover any damages—

WILLIAM LUX *Clk* — — —

THURSDAY 30th MAY 1754

The Commissioners met and were present

MR. THOMAS HARRISON   MR. WILLIAM ROGERS
MR. ALEXANDER LAWSON   DR WILLIAM LYON
MR. BRIAN PHILPOT JUNR—

Whereas there is a Vacancy by the Death of Colo. William Hammond and Major Thomas Sheredine two of the Commissioners of Baltimore Town, the Commissioners of Baltimore Town do therefore choose Nicholas Ruxton Gay and Mr. Loyd Buchanan as Commissioners in their Stead. Order'd that the clerk apply to the clerk of Baltimore County for a copy of the agreement between the Commissioners and John Ridgely for Building a Bridge: Order'd that the Clerk apply to Major Charles Ridgely for the Debt due from Edward Fotterell of 8£— Order'd that when any representation is made to the Clerk to enter any Lott fallen by neglecting to build thereon agreeably to act of Assembly that the said Clerk View the same and see that the representation be true 'fore he enter any such Lott— Order'd to write to Mr. John Ridgely to finish the Bridge according to his Agreement and his Letter of the 6th. february 1750 — —

Order'd to set up advertisements to inform all Proprietors of Lotts to enter their having complied with the act of Assembly obliging them to build a House to cover at Least four Hundred feet on their Respective Lotts — —

BALTIMORE TOWN JUNE 30th. 1768.

The Commissioners appointed by the act of Assembly entitled "an act for erecting a Court House and Public Prison for Baltimore County in the Town of Baltimore and for making sale of the old Court house and Prison met at the House of John Beal Bordly to consider of the putting the said act into Execution—

Present

JOHN B. BORDLEY . ROBERT ADAIR   ⎫
JOHN RIDGELY   ROBERT ALEXANDER ⎬ *Commissioners.*
JOHN MOALE   ANDREW BUCHANAN   ⎭

Memorandum Mr. William Smith a Commissioner had Notice but being sick coud not attend— The Commissioners agree that they will keep a Book and therein enter their proceedings— The subscription Papers being Produced are ordered to be entered and are as follows Viz : Here follows the Subscribers Names with the several Sums of money Subscribed towards the Building the Court house and Prison—in Balto Town Resolved immediately to set about collecting the Monies Subscribed for, and that Advertisements be published requesting payment to Mr. Andrew Buchanan who is with his Consent appointed Treasurer— The following advertisement was thereupon Signed by the Commissioners under named to be set up tomorrow— "The Subscribers towards building the New Court house and Prison are requested to pay their respective Subscriptions to Mr. Andrew Buchanan One of the Commissioners the Money being wanted in order to procure a Stock of Materials and for defraing immediate necessary Expenses preparative to the carrying on the said Buildings

Agreed to meet every Monday 6 oClock in the afternoon at Each Others houses by turns in Course as we are named in the act of Assembly—and as Much oftener as may be necessary upon Notice given— Alexander Wells having as we are informed offered to collect the Monies due on the 2d. and 3 being the lesser Subscription papers at 5 pr Cent We are of Opinion it is an advantageous offer the Subscriptions being dispersed in the Country, and therefore put a Copy of those Papers in the hands of Mr. Andrew Buchanan and desire he will agree with

Mr. Wells accordingly in the Name of the Commissioners: And also Copy of the first in Larger Paper for himself to receive by—together with the said three Original Subscriptions paper to be Safe Kept—

MONDAY JULY 11. 1768—

The Commissioners met at the House of Mr. John Ridgely

	JOHN B. BORDLY	ROBERT ALEXANDER
Present	JOHN RIDGELY	WILLIAM SMITH
	ROBERT ADAIR	ANDREW BUCHANAN

The Commissioners taking into Consideration the further execution of their Trust are of opinion it will be proper forthwith to procure and lay off the necessary Ground and to give Public Notice by advertisement that they think it Necessary to purchase Some of the Ground on the west side and on the East side of Calvert Street near the Top of the Hill at the head of the said Street and that they will Meet at the house of Robert Adair On Monday the 9th of August to Treat with the Proprietors for the Same. Notice is hereby given by the Commissioners That they thinking it necessary to purchase Some of the Ground on the East side and West side of Calvert Street being part of lotts Numbers 8. 11. 12. 137 and 138 adjoining the said Street in Baltimore Town do propose to meet at the house of Robert Adair Esquire in Balto Town on Monday the 8th. of August to treat with the proprietors thereof for the Same: if he or they shall think proper to attend for that purpose which if he or they omit to do the Commssrs. will proceed agreeable to the said Act of Assembly— Alexander Wells having agreed to collect the Monies On the 2d and 3d. Subscription papers on the Terms Mentioned in the Entry at the last meeting: Ordered that the Copies of the said Subscription Papers Signed by the Commissioners be delivered him With the following Authority indorsed thereon "We hereby authorise and Empower Alexander Wells to receive and collect the Several Sums Subscribed by the different Persons whose Names are Mentioned in this list and that he pay the Same to Andrew Buchanan One of the Commissioners"—which was accordingly indorsed signed by the Commissioners present and delivered Mr. Buchanan—It being intimated that Mr. William Lux is willing to assist the commsrs as a Clerk Gratis, Mr. John Ridgely is appointed to request his undertaking the same—

At a Meeting of the Comrs. at the house of Mr John Moale the 25 July 1768 present

JOHN RIDGELY   ROBERT ALEXANDER
JOHN MOALE   WILLIAM SMITH   ANDREW BUCHANAN

The Commissioners taking into consideration the further Execution of their trust do resolve that the public Prison be built of Stone not exceeding forty feet square and that the Court house be built of Brick not exceeding Sixty feet by forty feet— Ordered that Notice to given in Writing that the Commissioners will meet at the house of Mr Adair On Monday the 8th. day of August to contract with any Person or Persons for building and erecting the Goal in Baltimore Town agreeable to a Plan then to be produced and finding Materials for the Same— And also for Sinking and walling up a well and placing a Pump therein resolved that the Comrs. will meet on Monday Next at 9 oClock A M. and then proceed to lay out and ascertain the Ground as aforesaid—

MONDAY 8 AUGUST 1768 The Comrs. met   Present

JOHN RIDGELY   JOHN MOALE   ROBERT ADAIR
ROBERT ALEXANDER   WM SMITH   ANDR BUCHANAN

The Comrs. in further Execution of the Trust reposed in them proceeded with Surveyor of the County of Baltimore to run and lay out the Ground whereon to build the Court house and prison and did accordingly run out the Same— Mr Alexander Lawson appeared before the Commissioners and claimed as proprietor the land lying to the Eastward of Calvert street included in the said Survey and demanded the sum of 200£ runing Money as a Consideration for the Sale of his title to the said land—upon which the Comrs. taking into consideration the said offer are of opinion the said Sum is too exhorbitant. And no Person appearing to claim or make Sale of the Ground lying to the Westward of Calvert Street : resolved that a warrant be issued to the Sheriff of Baltimore County to Summon a Jury of freeholders to meet on Monday the to enquire as well who are the Owners of the said land to the Westward of Calvert Street as of the Value thereof and also of

the Value of the land lying to the Eastward of the said street.
and thereupon a Warrant was made out and Signed by the said
Comrs. The Comrs. appointed by act of Assembly entitled an
Act for erecting a Court house and Prison for Baltimore
County in Baltimore Town and for making the sale of the old
Court house and Prison— To the sheriff of Baltimore County
Greeting. You are hereby requested and commanded to return
a Jury of the most Substantial freeholders not less than twelve
inhabitants within your said County to be and appear before
Us on   the   day of   upon their Oaths to be by
us or the Major part of us then and there administered to enquire who is or are the Owner or Owners of the land by the
said Commrs. laid off next adjoining to Calvert Street at the
upper part thereof what is the Value thereof and what damages the owner or owners will sustain ; hereof fail not and have
you them there this Warrant : Given under our hands at Baltimore Town this 8th day of August. 1768.   Ordered that Notice
be given that the Commrs. will meet on Tuesday the   day
of this instant at the house of Robert Alexander and that the
Persons willing to contract agreeable to the former Advertisement do then deliver their proposals in Writing— So Ends
this sitting——

SATURDAY NOVEMBER 30th. 1776—

The Commissioners met and were present

> JOHN MOALE
> WILLIAM SMITH
> JOHN MERRYMAN

The Commissioners made choise of the following Persons
as officers for Baltimore town for the ensuing Year

EDWARD HANSON inspector of flour

JACOB KEEPORTS Corder of Wood

BASIL LUCAS corder of wood for Fells Point

JOHN FLANNAGAN Weigher of Hay

JOHN HART Clerk of the Markett

GEORGE WELSH Measurer of Grain etc

WILLIAM DUNKEN Culler of staves and Garbler of Shingles

THOMAS DONNELLON Guager of Liquors

There not being a Majority of Commissioners Present at
the Election Mr. Andrew Buchanan afterwards appeared and
acquissed in the Choise

10 SEPTEMBER 1779—

At a Meeting of the Commissioners of Baltimore Town September 10th. 1779.

Present JOHN MOALE
      ANDREW BUCHANAN
      JOHN MERRYMAN
      WILLIAM SMITH.

JOHN MCCLENNAN appointed weigher of Hay
HENRY LORAH appointed Clerk of the Markett
EDWARD HANSON appointed Inspector of Flour
JACOB KEEPORTS Wood Corder
JOHN HART Measurer of Grain Salt &c &c
JOHN MORRISON Culler of Staves &c — — —

BALTIMORE JANUARY 8th. 1781—

At a Meeting of the Commissioners for Baltimore Town present—

      ANDREW BUCHANAN
      JOHN MOALE
      THOMAS HARRISON
      WILLIAM SMITH.

When they proceeded to choose two Commissioners in the Place of Messrs. Robert Alexander and John Merryman whereupon Mr Richard Ridgely and Hercules Courtnay were chosen in the Rooms of Mr. Robert Alexander and Mr. John Merryman.

SATURDAY FEBRUARY 17th. 1781

Commissioners met.

      present
      WILLIAM SMITH
      JOHN MOALE
      HERCULES COURTNAY   Esquires—
      RICHARD RIDGELY

Commissioners met—

      present
      THOMAS HARRISON
      WILLIAM SMITH
      HERCULES COURTNAY
      RICHARD RIDGELY

Order'd that Henry Lorah John Hart and James Long on or before the third day of March next lay before the Commissioners a state of their transaction respectively while they acted as Clerk of Baltimore Market, and that they have Notice of this Order — —

SATURDAY MAY 26th. 1781—

Commissioners met

present

THOMAS HARRISON
JOHN MOALE
HERCULES COURTNAY
RICHARD RIDGELY

It is order'd that James Long clerk of the Market give Notice to the Butchers occupying stalls in the Market that after the 17th day of September next the stalls will be rented at forty shillings specie each—that what stalls are not occupied are to be immediately rented by the Clerk

All arreareges for Rent from the Butchers must be paid to the Clerk and in Case of Refusal the Names of such Persons so refusing are to be returned to the Commissioners who will proceed against the Defaulters—No Butcher is to occupy the stalls unless he agrees for them by the Year with the Clerk the Present Years Rent to be thirty Shillings Specie—

FRIDAY JULY 14 1781

Commissioners met.

Present

THOMAS HARRISON
JOHN MOALE
RICHARD RIDGELY
DANIEL BOWLEY — who qualified

according to Law before John Moale Esqur— —

The Commissioners having taken the Oath prescribed by Law relative to the choise of an Inspector of Flour in Baltimore Town and fells Point proceeded to the Choise of an Inspector to fill that office when David Moor was appointed and took the Oath Prescribed by the Constitution and Form of Government, and by the act to prevent the Growth of Toryism—

NOVEMBER 5. 1781

Present   THOMAS HARRISON
         WILLIAM SMITH
         JOHN MOALE
         DANL BOWLEY
         RD RIDGELY

Geo. Sewall Duglass appointed weigher of Hay upon taking
Oaths &c — -

RD CULVERWELL appointed Wood Corder
BAZIL NOALL appointed Measurer of Grain &c
JACOB DAWSON appointed Garbler, Culler of Staves &c
WILLIAM GIBSON appointed Clerk to ye Commissioners
DAVID MOOR appointed Inspector of Flour &c — —
Order'd that the Vendue Master pay to Such Person as the
Commissioners shall appoint, such sum as may be sufficient
to pay and Post the Market House and arround it—

                                    Adjourned—

THURSDAY NOVEMBER 15. 1781—

Present   THOMAS HARRISON
         JNO MOALE
         WILLIAM SMITH
         DAN BOWLEY
         HERCULES COURTNAY
         RD RIDGELY

Rd Culverwell having been an Indented Servant at the
Time prescribed by Law for taking the Oath of Allegiance to
the state, the Commissers had it administred to him and afterwards appointed him Wood-corder—at the Same Time the said
Culverwell declared his Belief in the Christian Religion.— —

FRIDAY NOV. 30. 1781—

At a Meeting of the commissioners .
Present   THOMAS HARRISON
         WILLIAM SMITH
         DANIEL BOWLEY
         RD RIDGELY

John Stoler appointed Clerk of the Market for Balto Town
for the Ensuing Year.

APRIL 24. 1782

Commissioners met

Present   THOMAS HARRISON
            WILLIAM SMITH
            DANL BOWLEY
            RD RIDGELY—   who agreeable
to the act of Assembly caused such part of Fells prospect to be
survey'd and laid out into Streets, Lanes and Alleys as will
appear by the Platt returned to the Clerk of Balto County
Court as well as One lodged by the said William Fell with the
Commissioners

The Commissioners of Baltimore Town met at the East
end thereof Called Fells Point the 16th May 1782.

Present   MR THOMAS HARRISON
            MR. JOHN MOALE
            MR HERCULES COURTNAY
            MR DANIEL BOWLEY

Messrs. Job Smith, William Trimble and Others inhabitants
of that part of the Town made application to have the Per-
mission and approbation of the Commissioners for filling up
the Hollows and lowering the high Grounds of Bond Street
and regulating the Same —The Commissioners are of the opinion that the Same is a Necessary work and that Messrs Job
Smith and William Trimble may remove the Earth from the
High Grounds between the Lotts of Mr. Johns and Mr. Collins
from one side of the Street to the Other for the Purpose of
filling up the Hollows and giving the said Street a Regular
descent or slope to carry of the Rain Water to pitt street
Southerly and North of the said Lotts to Lancaster alley.

The Deposition of Robert Long of Baltimore County who
being Sworn on the Holy Evangels of Almighty God before
the Commissioners of Baltimore Town deposeth and saith that
at the spot We now stand being at a Stone Marked E x M
No. 85 On Pitt street On the west side thereof deposeth and
saith that Sometime in the Year seventeen hundred and Sixty
three this Deponent came to Fells Point with a view to settle
and Purchase some lotts— That the Streets were Staked out at
the Corners by having two Stakes at Each corner and One

Stake between Every Lott—That this Deponent thinks that
Pitt Street at that time run into the Water ranging with the
said Stone mark'd as above, and a House built by a Certain
John and Robert Lowry now in the Tenure and Possession of
Mr. Jesse Hollingsworth— That this deponent assisted the
said Lowry in laying out the foundation of the said House
which they intended to do on the Street and that they ranged
with the Stakes above to fix the foundation as Near on the
Street as Possible— That Some Years afterwards this Deponent also assisted a Certain Alexander McMechen to lay
out the foundation of a House On the North East side of the
said street call'd Pitt Street which house was intended to be
built binding on the said Street— And this Deponent also
thinks that the said House was built on Pitt Street that the
inclosures now standing were erected as Near as possible where
the Stakes were Originally fixed as the Lines of the aforesaid
Street called Pitt street: to the Best of his Knowledge

Sworn to this 9th. day of
december 1782 before the   (Signed)   ROBERT LONG
Commissioners   of   Balto
Town

The Deposition of Thomas Bond son of John of Baltimore
County who being sworn on the Holy Evangels of almighty
God deposeth and Saith that above Nineteen Years ago the
Streets and Lotts being laid off on Fells Point he remembers
some of the stakes were standing and that the Range of houses
particularly the front of Mr Hollingsworth House the Paling
of Mr Purviances Lotts and a stone at Lott Number Eighty
five he believes to be as Near as possible on the south west side
of Pitt Street as formerly laid out by his father in addition to
Baltimore Town—

THOMAS BOND SON OF JOHN

The above deposition was taken and
Sworn to before John Moale one of the
Commissioners of Baltimore Town on the 10 of December 1782.

Signed   JOHN MOALE.

The Deposition of Mr. Thomas Bond, who being sworn on
the Holy Evangels of Almighty God deposeth and saith that
agreeable to the laying out of Fells point by his father as de-

scribed in the Deposition he made before the Commissioners of Baltimore Town on the Tenth day of December last Pitt street was continued quite into the Water and that Woolf street did not extend to the Water at the south End but ended in Pitt street and further this deponent saitheth not.

(Signed)

THOMAS BOND SON OF JOHN

The above Deposition taken before me
the Subscriber One of the Justices for Baltimore County this 8th day of January Seventeen hundred and Eighty three—

JOHN MOALE —

JUNE 26. 1782

Commissioners met

Present   THOMAS HARRISON   WILLIAM SMITH
           DANIEL BOWLEY   HERCULES COURTNAY

who agreeable to act of Assembly caused the Lotts of Land of John Moale and Andrew Stigar to be surveyed and laid out into Lotts and Streets as will appear by the Platt return'd to the Clerk of Baltimore County Court as well as One lodged by Said Moale and Stigar with the Commissioners—

At same Time Mr Moale agrees to open North street thro the Lott No. 82 which is left sufficiently wide, whenever the Proprietors of the land On high street will agree on their Parts to open it through to high Street.

JULY 9th, 1782   Commissioners met

Present   THOMAS HARRISON
           WILLIAM SMITH
           DANIEL BOWLEY
           HERCULES COURTNAY
           RICHARD RIDGELY

The Commissioners having taken the Oath prescribed by act of Assembly proceeded to the Election of an Inspector of flour for Baltimore Town and made choise of David Moore who is directed to qualify himself accordingly

JULY 8th, 1783—

Commissioners met
    Present
      WILLIAM SMITH
      DANIEL BOWLEY
      HERCULES COURTNAY
   and RD RIDGELY

who made choise of David Moor for inspector for the ensuing year

SEPTEMBER 11. 1783—

Commissioners met
    Present
      JOHN MOALE
      WILLIAM SMITH
      HERCULES COURTNAY
      RD RIDGELY

Mr. Jno. Sterett heretofore chosen a Commissioner qualified himself as such by taking the Oath faithfully to execute the office of commissioner of Baltimore Town Mr. John Robert Hollyday and Thomas Russell having applied to the Commissioners for having the following streets and alleys open'd and Made Public as an High Way thro their Lotts, the Commissioners made the following order to wit—that a street Thirty three feet wide shoud be extended from Baltimore Street to East Lane parallel with Gay Street begining at the End of Three hundred and Eleven feet west in Baltimore Street from the intersection of Gay Street and Baltimore Street The Commissioners also consented that East Lane shoud be open'd and made forty feet wide by adding ground on the North side of East Lane from North Lane to gay Street—

The Commissioners open'd a street called Hollyday Street of Eighty feet wide begining for the Same at the End of two hundred and Eighty Two feet west from the intersection of Gay street and East street as enlarged and runing North parallel with gay street three hundred and twelve feet and One half foot.

The Commissioners open'd an alley called orange alley of Eighteen feet wide begining for the same at the End of One hundred and Ninty four feet north on Gay Street from the intersection of Gay Street and East street as above enlarged and runing thence parallel with East Street of the same width till it intersects Hollyday Street—

The Commissioners being met are of opinion that Calvert street shoud have the same width in its extention south into the Basin as it has at its intersection with Baltimore Street which width we find by the Records of the Town to be four Perches and we further certify that from the Best Evidence we cou'd collect and the Most exact Measurement We, are of opinion that the West front of Mr. Skinnors Ennals House is properly fixed on the East side of Calvert street.

Given under our hands at Baltimore 16th. of December 1783.   JOHN MOALE
                 DANIEL BOWLEY
                 HERCULES COURTNAY   } Commissioners
                 RD. RIDGELY

Baltimore County to wit—

Whereas the subscribers Thomas Yates Proprietor of the ground on the South side of the Causeway from the west Side of Eden Street and Peter Litig and the said Thomas Yates proprietors of the grounds on the North side of the said Causeway being desirous that wilkes street shoud be extended across the Causeway to Philpots point have permitted that the same shall be extended of the same width to the Point of Philpots as the said street   Now We the Subscribers the said Thomas Yates and Peter Littig do hereby agree and bind Ourselves that the said Street shall be extended at the Width of wilkes street to Philpots Point and that the Same when compleated and extended shall be the Limits and bounds of our Grounds and Lands as aforesaid and that we will not stop up the said street when made out at any Time hereafter: Witness our hands and Seals this Twenty fourth day of April 1784.

THOMAS YATES [SEAL]
PETER LITTIG [SEAL]

Witness
      ROBERT CAMPBELL
      EDWARD DAY

BALTIMORE TOWN 16th. JUNE 1784

The Commissioners of said Town met and where Present
WILLIAM SMITH   RICHARD RIDGELY
DANIEL BOWLEY   HERCULES COURTNAY

The Deposition of Mark Alexander Senr. taken before the said Commissioners as follows to wit

That Some time in the years 1769 or 1770 when this Deponent was building his wharehouses near the County wharf
there was an agreement made between this Deponent and a
certain Nicholas Hassellback who own'd and was possess'd
of a Lott of Ground westward of this Deponents Lott that there
shoud be a dock left open between this Deponent's Lotts and
Said Hassellback's Lott of Sixteen feet wide: That this Deponent agreed to give ten feet of his ground, and said Hassellback agreed to give Six feet of his ground for the purpose of
Keeping open said Dock— That This deponent agreeable to
said Agreement built his said wharehouses ten feet Eastward
of the Boundary of his said Lotts and that he at Sundry Times
since the said wharehouses were built clean'd the said Dock,
and occupied it with Scows and other Small Craft forever afterwards while he continued to possess and hold the said wharehouses &c and that there never was after any Dispute or Mur-
mering about the Same by or with the said Hassellback or
any other Person respecting the Same.

Signed MARK ALEXANDER

I do hereby certify that Mark Alexander in Presence of the
Town Commissioners made Oath on the Holy Evangels of
Almighty God to the aforegoing deposition and signed the
Same before me

[SIGNED] THOMAS RUSSELL

Upon the Evidence aforesaid it is order'd and adjudged by
the Commissioners aforesaid that the Dock aforesaid for the
width of sixteen Feet wide shall always hereafter be left open
as an high way in a South direction according to the agreement aforesaid

WILLIAM SMITH   HERCULES COURTNAY
DANIEL BOWLEY   RD. RIDGELY

JULY 6, 1784

The commissioners met

Present

WILLIAM SMITH
HERCULES COURTNAY
DANIEL BOWLEY
RD RIDGELY

The Commissioners according to act of Assembly took into
consideration the choice of officers for the Town of Baltimore

when having Qualified they chose George Lowderman for Wood corder for that Part of Baltimore Town called Fells Point

Rd Culverwell was appointed Wood Corder for Baltimore Town — David Moore was appointed inspector of Flour in Baltimore Town—

John Morrison and Timothy *Fleiar appointed Garbler of Staves — —

OCTOBER 4. 1784

The Commissioners met

Present   JOHN MOALE
HERCULES COURTNAY
JOHN STERETT
DANIEL BOWLEY   }   *Esquires.*

Mr. William Goodwin heretofore chosen a commissioner in the Room of Thomas Jones Esqr. (who has resigned) qualified himself as such by taking the Oath faithfully to execute the office of Commissioner of Baltimore Town

BALTIMORE TOWN FEBRUARY 4th. 1785.

Commissioners met   Present

WILLIAM SMITH   WILLIAM GOODWIN   RICHD. RIDGELY
JOHN STERETT   DANIEL BOWLEY

The Commissioners appointed to erect a Market house on that part of Baltimore Town call'd Harrison's Marsh produced a Bond obligating themselves to erect the said Market House according to the Plan to the Said Bond annexed which Bond and Plan was approved of and Order'd to be filed—

FEBRUARY 5 1785.

The Commissioners met

JOHN MOALE   JOHN STERETT
Present   WM SMITH   WM GOODWIN
DANL. BOWLEY   RD RIDGELY
HERCULES COURTNAY

Leonard Harbaugh, William Hammond, William Goodwin Jonathan Hudson and Loyd Goodwin appeared and laid before the Commissioners a plan for erecting a Market house on the west side of the Bason persuant to act of Assembly—which

---

*This name is difficult to decipher in original; hence is open to question.

plan was approved of and Bond was taken to compleat and Erect the Same accordingly— Thomas Yates and Peter Littig having applied to the Commissioners together with John Hammond who are the proprietors of the Ground situate on the Causeway between Caroline Street and Philpots Point to Extend wilkes Street in a due direction of its present Width to Philpots Hill the said space of Ground with the consent of the said Proprietors is hereby condemned and Opened as a Street and high way for the use of the public for Ever hereafter — —

APRIL 1st 1785

The Commissioners met	Present
WILLIAM SMITH	HERCULES COURTNAY
DANIEL BOWLEY	RICHD. RIDGELY

The Commissioners appointed Mr. Jacob Towson their Clerk and agreed to give him a Sallery of fifty Pounds for One Year Order'd that the Clerk give Notice in the Public Papers that the Commissioners of Baltimore Town intend to meet on the 23rd day of next Month to carry into Execution the act entitled "an act "to empower the Commissioners of Baltimore Town to make a Correct Survey of said Town and for other Purposes therein mentioned of which all persons in anywise interested are requested to take Notice: Order'd that the Clerk give Notice in the public Papers that the Commissioners of Balto. Town will meet at Mr. De'Witts Coffee House on Monday 11th. Instant at Eleven OClock to Contract with Proper Persons as constables and watchmen where all Persons desirous of undertaking said offices are requested to make application in Person at the Meeting and bring with them recommendations of their good Character— Order'd that the Clerk be empower'd to contract for Twelve watch Houses of four feet square and six and a half feet high with a Door a lock and Key to Each————

At a Meeting of the Commissioners of Baltimore Town on Monday the Eleventh of April 1785 agreeable to advertisements for the Purpose of appointing constables and watchmen to watch the Town—

	JOHN MOALE	HERCULES COURTNAY
Present	WM SMITH	JOHN STERETT
	WM GOODWIN	DANIEL BOWLEY

RESOLVED that the Town be divided into Six Wards or Districts as follows—

No 1. comprehending all that Part of the Town south of Pratt Street.— ' 2 comprehending all that Part of the Town north of Pratt Street and West of Charles— 3 comprehending all East of Charles street and west of South stret— 4 comprehending all East of south street west of Jones's Falls 5 comprehending all East of Jones Falls and west of harford street 6 comprehending all East of Harford street.

RESOLVED that Constables be appointed for the Town to whom we will pay 5£ pr Month — — also 14 watchmen who shall be entitled to 4£ pr Month The Constables appointed are Captain Daniel Dennis, Samuel Chester and Henry Robinson— The watchmen appointed are

1 Jacob Keller	4 Richard Bear	7 John German
2 John Silvester	5 Henry Kain	8 Dennis Sheakeley
3 Hugh Neale	6 James Dugan	9 Lewis Stout
10 John Bready	11 Nath. Aldridge	12 Hugh Seward

Mr. Gibson having applied to the Commissioners of Baltimore Town by order of Baltimore County Court for the use of the Rooms over the Market House to lodge the County records in whils't the Arches are making under the Court house it is agreed that Mr Gibson shall have the use of the said Rooms for the purpose aforesaid at Seven Pounds Ten Shillings pr. Month. The Time to Commence from the delivery of the Keys and to Continue untill the Market house is to be sold: Mr. Gibson to have three Months Notice of the Time of Sale in Order to Deliver up the House

MAY 14th. 1785.

James Brown exhibited his account for making and painting thirteen Centry Boxes for the Watchmen of Baltimore Town amount 89. 12. 6. and prayed an Order on the sheriff for the Same which was allowed and Accordingly Given him and his receipt taken for the Same—

23 MAY 1785—

The Commissioners met this day according to Notices

JNO MOALE	WM. GOODWIN ⎫
WM SMITH	JNO. STERETT ⎬ *Comrs.*
HERCULES COURTNAY	DAN: BOWLEY ⎭

The Business of the Meeting being to appoint a Surveyor or Surveyors to make an accurate survey and Platt of the Town of Baltimore agreeably to an act of Assembly past the last session for that Purpose the application of Geo: Goldsmith Presbury and Zachariah McCubbin for that appointment were received and read; The Commissioners agree to employ the said Presbury and McCubbin to make a Survey and Platt aforesaid in the following manner Mr. Presbury to make a Survey of that part of the Town to the Eastward of

and Mr. McCubbin to make a Survey of all that Part of the Town westward and Southward of the west side of

So that the two Platts when returned shall fit and Compose a General and compleat Survey of the whole ——

7 JUNE 1785

The Commissioners met   present

WM SMITH   RICHARD RIDGELY
DANIEL BOWLEY   JOHN STERETT

The Commissioners on application and with Consent of the Proprietors of the lotts Numbers 45 and 48 Situate in Baltimore Town have opened a Lane by condemning that part of the lott No 48 which lies on the West side of a Line extended South parallel with light lane and Calvert Street from the South West Corner of lott No. 47 to the south End of lott No. 48 and the said Parcel of Ground so as aforesaid Condemned for Public use is hereby declared to be a High way for the use of the Public forever hereafter—

It is further ordered that all Nuisances and Obstructions on the said Parcel of Ground shall be removed in Order that the Same be free and uninterupted as a Passage and high way hereafter and that George Prestman Peter Hoffman Edward Dorsey John McHenry and Cyprian Wells or any three of them be empowered and directed to remove any Nuisances or obstructions in the said lane so condemned or any Part of it—

R RIDGELY *Clk p. Tem*

18 AUGST 1785   The Commissioners met   Present

JNO. MOALE.   RICHARD RIDGELY ⎫
DAN: BOWLEY   JNO. STERETT ⎬ *Comrs.*
                                              ⎭

Thomas Elliott appointed a Commissioner in the room of Hercules Courtnay Esquire who has resigned—Ordered that the Clerk of the Commissioners advertise and give Public Notice that the Commissioners of Baltimore Town will meet on the 15th, day of October next and sell to the highest bidder the old Market house with the Buildings thereon laid off into convenient lotts according to the act of Assembly passed Last Session — — Ordered that the Clerk receive from the sheriff One hundred Pounds ten Shillings and three Pence part of the Eighteen penny Tax to pay the watchmen a Months wages due the 11th. instant and Other Expenses attending the watch as pr. account and that the Clerk keep fair accounts of the receipts and Expenditures of all Monies and a Particular return of the Services and pay of the watchmen—

15th SEPTEMBER 1785   The Commissioners met present

WM. SMITH	DAN. BOWLEY	} Comrs.
WM. GOODWIN	THOMAS ELLIOTT	

Thomas Elliott having previously qualified as a Commissioner in the Room of Hercules Courtnay Esq. who had resigned — — The New Market on Howard Hill being this day opened the Comrs. appoint Septimus Noel Clerk of the said Market who shall be allowed thirty pounds for this Present year. It is resolved that the Stalls in the Said Market shall be let at three Pounds p Annum payable Quarterly— The accounts for watching the street the last Month ending the 11th. Instant amounting to £88.19.10 is allowed and the Clerk is directed to call on the Sheriff for that amount and discharge the same

Baltimore 17 September 1785 Came Septimus Noel before me the Subscriber and qualified according to law to perform the office of Clerk for Howard Hill with Justice and Integrity—

L. S. LYDE GOODWIN

OCTOBER 3rd. 1785.

The Commissioners met—Present

DAN BOWLEY	}
WM. GOODWIN	} Comrs.
THOMAS ELLIOTT	}

They opened the Polls for two delegates to represent this Town in the General Assembly and three Comptrollers for Baltimore Town and adjourned to the 4th Int.

OCTOBER 4th. 1785

The Commissioners Met—   Present — —

JNO MOALE   THOMAS ELLIOT }
DAN BOWLEY   WM. GOODWIN   } Comrs.

When David McMechen and John Sterett Esquires were unanimously Chosen delegates to the Assembly and Thomas Russell James Calhoun and Lyde Goodwin were elected Comptrollers—

OCTOBER 6th. 1785

Commissioners met   Present

JNO. MOALE   DAN BOWLEY }
THOMAS ELLIOTT   R RIDGELY } Comrs
WM. GOODWIN   }

The sale of the old Market House agreeably to the platt hereto annexed being postponed to this day the Commissioners proceeded to adjust the Terms of sale which are that one third be paid in Ten days one third in three Months and One third in Six Months the purchasers giving Bond with Security and no title to be given the purchaser or purchasers until the whole purchase Money be paid— Possession to be delivered on the first payment — If default be made in any of the payments the purchaser or Purchasers to pay Ten pr Cent— The purchaser entitled to the improvements On the premises, but that part of the said improvement which is built on in the street to be removed in Ten days after Possession shall be given; the Materials to belong to the purchaser of the Lotts from which they were removed— The Lotts are subject to a Ground rent of one shilling and three pence Sterling Pr foot.

15 October 1785.

The Commissioners Met   Present

JNO MOALE   WM SMITH   }
WM. GOODWIN   JOHN STERETT } Comrs.

The Accounts for Watching the Streets the last Month Ending the 11th Inst. Amounting to £92.2.3. is allowed and the clerk is desired to call on the Sheriff for amount of that Sum and discharge the same. —— ——

BALTIMORE 22nd OCTOBER 1785

Commissioners met   Present

JNO. MOALE   THOMAS ELLIOT
DAN BOWLEY   RICHARD RIDGELY
WM. GOODWIN   WM. SMITH

The center Market on Jones's Falls being to be opened on Wednesday Next Captain Dennis on application is appointed clerk of the said Market for the ensuing year and to be allowed Thirty Pounds for his services— The Stalls to be let at three pounds Each to the Butchers who are to take their Stands at the End of the Market next Baltimore Street on Each Side untill all are supplied paying one half of the stall rent in hand which the clerk of the Market is authorised to receive— Gardners and People who supply the Market with Vegetables choosing to take Stalls at the same rate may be accomodated at the lower end of the upper Market begining at Second Street and proceeding upwards towards the Butchers Stalls or Stands — The Country People to be accomodated in the lower Market between second Street and Water Street to take their stands in the House as they come to Market — —

Messrs. Thomas Russell and Jno Hammond who were nominated by the Commissioners to collect the Money levied upon the proprietors of Grounds on Hanover Street and Lane for opening the Same into a Street report that they have received of the said Money to the amount of three hundred Pounds: And as it appears that several of the Proprietors have neglected to pay the said Thomas Russell and Jno Hammond are directed to apply to a Lawyer and Order suits to be commenced agreeably to the Powers Given the Commissioners by the law for opening the said Lane — —

9 DECEMBER 1785

The Commissioners met   Present

JNO MOALE   DAN BOWLEY } Comrs.
WM SMITH   RICHD RIDGELY }

The Accounts for Watching the Streets the last Month Ending the 11th. of November last amounting to £93.4.3 is allowed and the Clerk is desired to call on Wm. McLaughlin Esquire Collector for that Amount and discharge the Same ——

24 December 1785

The Commissioners met   Present

JNO MOALE   JNO STERET }
WM SMITH   WM GOODWIN }*Comrs*

The accounts for Watching the Streets the last Month Ending the 11th. Instant amounting to £90.17.6 is allowed and the Clerk is desired to call On William McLaughlin Esquire collector for the Amount and to discharge the Same—

11th FEBRUARY 1786.—

The Commissioners met   Present

JNO MOALE   RICHD RIDGELY }
WM SMITH   WM GOODWIN }*Comrs—*

The Accounts for Watching the streets from 11th. december 1785 to this day inclusive Amounting to £210.15.6 is allowed and the Clerk is desired to call on William McLaughlin Esquire Collector for that amount and discharge the Same.— —

18 MARCH 1786

The Commissioners met   Present

WM GOODWIN   RICHD RIDGELY }
JNO STERETT   DAN : BOWLEY }*Comrs.*

The Accounts for watching and lighting the Streets &c from the 11th. february to the 11th. March Inst. Inclusive amounting to £87.12.9 is allowed and the Clerk is desired to call on Wm. McLaughlin Esquire Collector for that sum and discharge the Same — —

MAY 16. 1786

The Commissioners met   Present

WM SMITH   RICHD. RIDGELY }
JNO STERETT   DAN BOWLEY }*Comrs.*

On application of the Proprietors of the lotts situate on the East side of Walnut Street from Pratt Street to Barre Street to have the Same Stopped up and the Commissioners on Examination of the Platt thereof being of the opinion that Neither the public or any Individual wou'd be injured thereby — It is therefore Ordered that the said Street called Walnut Street be and is hereby abolished and Stopped up and that Each Person interested by having lotts on the street aforesaid be entitled to One half of said Street on Each side and that Battle alley be opened from Howard street to Sharp street —

JUNE 1st 1786—

The Commissioners met   Present

JNO MOALE   THOMAS ELLIOTT   DAN : BOWLEY ⎱ *Comrs.*
WILLIAM SMITH   WM GOODWIN   ⎰

The Commissioners being requested by the Vestry of St Pauls Parish to fix the Bounds and Limits of the Church Lands Viz the East Line in front of the New Church dividing the Original Lotts Nos. 18. 19. 20. The Said line is fixed to begin On Charles Street at the South West Corner of the Stone wall laid for the foundation of the New Church yard and runs thence Easterly 21½ perches parrallel to the front wall of the New Church and Eleven feet from the Same untill it intersects St Pauls lane as Originally laid out.

17th. JULY 1786—

The Commissioners met   Present

JNO. MOALE   DANL. BOWLEY ⎱ *Comrs.*
WM SMITH   RICHD. RIDGELY ⎰

The Commissioners proceeded to the appointment of an Inspector of Flour and David Moor was Elected for that Purpose—

George Sewall Duglass appointed Weigher of hay—Richard Moale is appointed Clerk to the Commissioners with a Sallery of Thirty five Pounds p Annum—And Samuel Chester Constable of the Watch— Order Given to Daniel Dennis On William McLaughlin Esquire for £85.11.9 Specie for one Months wages due the Watch Ending the 11th. Inst.

31st. AUGST. 1786—

The Commissioners agreeably to their Notice of the Twenty Sixth of August Met at Fells Point Market House—

Present   JNO. MOALE   ⎫
          THOMAS ELLIOT   ⎬ *Comrs.*
          WILLIAM GOODWIN ⎭

But there not being a Sufficient Number of the Members of the Board present to proceed to Business adjourned their Meeting to the Wednesday following being the 6th. of September following   —   —   —

6th. SEPTEMBER 1786—

The Commissioners met agreeably to adjournment of the 31 Augst. at Mrs. Balls Coffee house present

JNO. MOALE
THOMAS ELLIOT   }Comrs.
DANIEL BOWLEY

But there not being a Sufficient Number of the Board present to proceed to Business gave Orders that a Notice be given in hand Bills setting forth their Meeting on Thursday the 14th Sepr at Fells Point Market house————

SEPTEMBER 14. 1786—

Agreeable to the Notice in hand Bills of the 6th. Inst. the Commissioners met at Fells point Market house   Present

JNO. MOALE   WM SMITH   }Esqrs. Comrs.
DAN: BOWLEY   WILLIAM GOODWIN

The Commissioners then proceeded to fix the location and Boundaries of the Several Lotts on Fells Point agreeably to an Act of Assembly made for that Purpose begining at the Corner of Market Square at a Corner Stone known by the Name of Enloe's Corner runing down Alsiana Street to Street thence down   Street to a Corner Stone Known by the Name of   in Order to fix Market Square and from thence to regulate the adjoining Lotts—Then the Commissioners after fixing Market Square adjourned—

4 OCTOBER 1786

The Commissioners met   Present

JNO MOALE   WM SMITH   DAN BOWLEY }Comrs.—
THOS. ELLIOT   WM GOODWIN   RD. RIDGELY

On the application of Saml. and Robert Purviance and Jno. McLure it is hereby Ordered that Commerce Street be and is hereby declared to be a Street and Public highway forever hereafter for the use of the public, and that the Same shall be taken and Considered as a street for Public use at all Times hereafter pursuant to the powers in the said Comrs. Vested by Virtue of the Act of Assembly for that purpose made and provided.—

20th. NOVEMBER 1786—

The Commissioners met   Present

JOHN MOALE   WM SMITH } Comrs.
THOMAS ELLIOTT   DAN BOWLEY }

Upon application of Sundry Inhabitants of the East End of Balto Town We do appoint Peter Weary wood-Corder for Fells Point and Thomas Trimble Clerk of that Market for One Year the said Clerk to be allowed twenty pounds Current Money and the Wood Corder such Charge for Cording as the Act of Assembly under which we appoint him directs — —

16 FEBRUARY 1787

At a Meeting of the Commissioners   Present

JOHN MOALE   WM GOODWIN } Comrs.
WM SMITH   DAN BOWLEY }

Resolved that the Eighteen Penny Tax allowed by Law for Watching and lighting the Streets of Baltimore be levied and Assessed on the Inhabitants of the Town for the year Seventeen hundred and Eighty Six— Ordered that the Clerk give the Collector of the said Tax a Copy of the above Resolve ———

MARCH 15th 1787

At a Meeting of the Commissioners   Present

JNO MOALE WILLIAM SMITH RD. RIDGELY DAN BOWLEY and THOMAS ELLIOT

Major Nathaniel Smith was Elected Inspector of Salted Provisions for the Town of Baltimore agreeably to an Act of Assembly passed November Session 1786 and that the Clerk give Notice of the appointment

Resolved that this Board will meet on the first Monday in April to Settle with Watch and then discharge them if the Funds which are appropriated for carrying them on are insufficient or cannot be collected.— —

Ordered that the Clerk call on the Vendue Master for his accounts and receive from him whatever Balance may be due under the law for watching and lighting the Town — — — — —

3rd. APRIL 1787.

The Commissioners met　　Present

JNO. MOALE　　　　　DAN BOWLEY' ⎰
WM SMITH　　　　　　RD. RIDGELY　⎱ *Comrs.*

The Commissioners being called on by Doctor Boyd to fix the Corner at the intersection of North and East lane, and the Corner at the intersection of East lane and Calvert Street have caused a Stone to be put up 16½ feet West from the North West Corner of a Brick Stable on the Corner of Lott No 5 and Owned by Thomas Russell Esqr. for the intersection of the two lanes aforesaid and have also caused a Stone to be put up at the South west Corner of Lott No 9 allowing forty feet in addition to Calvert Street for the Court house Space as before fixed — —

3rd APRIL 1787 P M—

The Commissioners met　　Present

JNO. MOALE　　　　　RICHD. RIDGELY ⎰
WM SMITH　　　　　　DANL. BOWLEY　⎱ *Comrs.*

Received from Thomas Yates Auctioneer his accounts of Town duties made up to the 20th. of January 1787 Amounting to Seven hundred and Seventy five pounds two Shillings and One penny as per. Account filed — — —

Thomas Donnellan appointed Gauger of Liquors for Baltimore Town under the act of Assembly of 1784 and he qualified in Presence of the Commissioners before Jno. Moale Esquire by taking the Oath prescribed by Law— —

　　Jno Weatherburn appointed Wood Corder for Baltimore Town

　　James Long appointed Clerk of the Market called the Center Market

11th. APRIL 1787

The Commissioners met　　Present

JNO MOALE　　　　　　RD RIDGELY
WILLIAM SMITH　　　　DAN BOWLEY

The Commissioners drew an order on the auctioneer Thomas Yates at sight in favor of their Clerk for four hundred and thirty four Pounds One Shilling and Eleven pence with particular directions that if it was not paid in three days to have the Same protested before a Notary Public — — —

12 APRIL 1787—

The Commissioners met   Present

JNO MOALE   DAN BOWLEY   ⎰
WM SMITH   THOMAS ELLIOT ⎱ *Comrs.*

Ordered that the Clerk draw an Order on the Treasurer of
the Western Shore of Maryland in the Name of the Commissioners of Baltimore Town for the Surplus of the funds appropriated for the use of St. John College and allowed the
Town of Baltimore by an Act of Assembly passed November
Session 1784

4th. JUNE 1787

The Commissioners met   Present

JNO. MOALE   DAN BOWLEY ⎰
WM SMITH   RD. RIDGELY ⎱ *Comrs.*

The Commissioners then proceeded to appoint a Wood-
Corder when Jno. Gottro was Chosen— Ordered that the
Clerk give Notice of this appointment

Resolved that the pay of the Watchmen be 3£ pr Month
from the 11th of June 1787 until the 11th. of September following and four Pounds pr Month from the 11th. September 1787
to the 11th. of April 1788— Ordered that Captain Dennis do
immediately discharge John George Everheart for misbe-
haviour —

JUNE 19th. 1787 —

The Commissioners met   Present

JNO MOALE   WM. GOODWIN ⎰
WM SMITH   DANL BOWLEY ⎱ *Comrs.*

Ordered that the Clerk call on Jno. Staler formerly Clerk
of the Market for his account— On Daniel Dennis late Clerk
of the Marsh Market for his account and On Septimus Noel
and James Long Present Clerks of the Marsh and Hill Markets for their respective accounts— Major Thomas Yates
Auctioneer for Baltimore Town produced his account of Sales
of the old Market House which was ordered to be recorded

as follows— Sales at Vendue of the old Market House the
7th. of October 1785 for acct. of Momrs. of Baltimore Town

No 1 one lott as pr Platt...R. Ridgely ....£ 330.0.—
 2 one do .... Chas. Myers .... 280.0.—
 3 one do .... Wm. Hammond .... 375.0.—
 4 one do .... Cyprian Wells ..... 330.0.—
 5 one do .... A and A Robinson.. 210.0.—
 6 one do .... Wm Hammond 410.0.0

           £1935.0.0—

charges Viz

Thomas Yates his Commission on ⎱
 Sales One pr Ct as pr Agree- ⎰ " 19.7——
ment ....

Cash pd G. G Presbury for Platts..... 15.

Rd. Ridgely for a deduction of this ⎱
sum the lott No 1 being purchased
in for acct. of Comrs. at the day of ⎰ 50.2.0
sale and Since sold By R. Ridgely to ————
Jno. Wells for £300............. 70.4.0

     N Proceed £1864.16.0

At the Same time the Executors of Thomas Harrison deceased Exhibited their account for Ground rent of the old
Market house with The Commissioners of the Town and it
was also ordered to be recorded—which is as follows Viz—

The Commissioners of Balto Town

   To the Exrs of Thomas Harrison deceased Dr.
 1782 ⎱   Sterling.
March 25 ⎰ To amt. of Ground rent due Thos⎱
     Harrison on the Market House Lott to ⎰£18.18.2
     this date........................

 1785 ⎱
Octr. 7th ⎰ To 3 years 7 Months Ground rent on⎱
     ditto to this date when sold at 8£ Sterg ⎰£28.13.6
     Pr Annum......................

            £47.11.8

 £47.11.8 Sterg @ 66 2-3....is £79.6.0 Currency. ——

The Commissioners gave an Order on Major Thomas Yates to the Commissioners for Building the Center Market house for £1345.4 being the Proportion of the Nt. Proceeds of the above account of sales due to that Market — — — — The Commissioners also gave an Order on Major Thomas Yates to the Com m srs for Building Hanover Market House for £451.8— being the Proportion of the Nt Proceeds of the above acount of Sales due that Market — — They also gave to the Executors of Thomas Harrison deceased an Order On Major Thomas Yates for £79.6 — Currency being the amt of Ground rent due on the Old Market House to Thomas Harrison the day of Sale — — —

JULY 2nd. 1787—

At a Meeting of the Commissioners   Present

WM SMITH	WM. GOODWIN
DAN : BOWLEY	THOMAS ELLIOT

Comrs.

Jacob Keeports is appointed Wood-Corder for Baltimore Town untill the 10th. day of November Next—and David Moor Inspector of flour for One year from this date— Same day Jacob Keeports qualified before G. Goldsmith Presbury Esquire faithfully to Execute and Perform the said office agreeably To the form and directions of an Act of Assembly for that Purpose made and provided which qualification is filed among the records of the Comrs of the Town— Resolved that the Clerks of the Several Markets may and are hereby Authorised to rent to the Vendors of Either fresh or Salted Provisions Such Stalls in the Markets as are not already occupied by the Butchers—

JULY 16th. 1787.

The Commissioners met   Present

WM SMITH	DAN BOWLEY
WM GOODWIN	RICHD. RIDGELY

Comrs.

On the Petition of the Proprietors holding lotts on the East and West side of light lane, that the Same may be opened for the Space of Eleven feet on Each Side of said lane and Converted into a Street to be called Light Street — It is therefore Ordered that the said lane shall forever hereafter be Kept open as an high way of the width of Thirty Eight feet and a half adding Eleven feet on Each side of said lane and that the Same shall be forever hereafter Kept open for the Purpose of an high way to be called Light Street reserving that Part of the West side thereof where Nicholas Rogers Esqr. has a Brick house at the Corner of Baltimore Street —

26 AUGUST 1787

Commissioners met   Present

JNO MOALE   WM SMITH   THOS. ELLIOT } Comrs.
DAN BOWLEY   RD. RIDGELY

Thomas Yates Auctioneer was called before the Commissioners to answer why the Town duties were not paid to their Clerk agreeably to their Orders— Upon his faithful Promiss to discharge them in the Course of Six days he was discharged— Jno Merryman Esqr. was Elected a Commissioner in the Place of Jno. Sterett Esq.—deceased— Thomas Bailey appointed Clerk of Fells Point Market House——

20th. JANUARY 1788—

At a meeting of the Commissioners of Baltimore Town— Present

JOHN MOALE   RD. RIDGELY
WM SMITH   DAN BOWLEY   } Comrs.
WM GOODWIN   THOMAS ELLIOT

It was Resolved that the Eighteen Penny tax allowed by Law for the watching and lighting the Town of Baltimore be levied and assessed on the Inhabitants of the said Town for the Year Seventeen hundred and Eighty Seven— Ordered that the Clerk of the Commissioners furnish the Collector of the Town Tax with the above resolve ——

MARCH 24th. 1788—

At a Meeting of the Commissioners   Present

JNO MOALE WM GOODWIN DAN BOWLEY } Esqrs. Comrs.
WM SMITH RD. RIDGELY   THOMAS ELLIOT

Resolved that Public Notice be given in both the News papers that on Monday the first day of April next the Polls will be opened by the Commissioners of Baltimore Town agreeably to an Act of Assembly for the purpose of holding an Election for delegates to represent this Town in the Convention to be held at the City of Annapolis for the purpose of considering the newly Proposed Constitution or Plan of a Federal Goverment—

23 JUNE 1788— (omitted)

The Commissioners met   Present

Wm Smith   John Moale ⎱ Comrs.
Wm Goodwin   Dan Bowley ⎰

The Commissioners being called upon by the Proprietors
of the Lotts between Front Street and high Street opposite
the Bridge in Baltimore Street (commonly called Philpots
Bridge) and the lotts on the south side of York Street between high Street and Exeter Street, in Order that a Public
Street may be opened through the same Agreeably to the
Platt thereof filed by this Board Ordered that the Same be
condemned as a Public Street and High way forever Agreeably to the Platt thereof, and that it be recorded as Such in
the Records of this Town ———

3rd JULY 1788—

The Commissioners met at Fells Point   Present

Jno. Moale   Thomas Elliot ⎱ Comrs.
Wm Smith   Danl. Bowley   ⎰

The Commissioners being called on by Peter Carr and Henry
Datur to ascertain the Corner of Intersection of Thames Street
and Bond Street on the West side thereof and having caused
the Street to be Measured from Lancaster alley along the West
side of Bond Street to the South East Corner of George
Wells New Brick house Do fix the said Corner of Wells's
House as the Boundary at the aforesaid intersection—
The Commissioners find from Measuring Bond Street from
Abraham Enloes Corner (which hath been proved and ad-
mitted to be right) that there appears a deficiency of Three
feet and a Half between that and the above Mentioned Corner
of Thames and Bond Streets and as the Same cannot remidied
otherwise than by Making Lancaster Alley so much narrower
between Bond Street and the Water without altering the Situation of a Great Number of houses along the said Bond Street
and causing much Confusion, Therefore establish the Width
of lancaster alley between Bond Street and the Water to be
Thirty Six feet and a half.——

5th JULY 1788.

The Commissioners met   Present

Jno Moale   Richd. Ridgely   ⎫
                                        ⎬ Comrs.
                     Dan Bowley   ⎮
Wm Smith   Thomas Elliot   ⎭

David Moor was at this Meeting appointed Inspector of

flour for the Ensuing year: who is required to qualify as such according to act of Assembly The Commissioners then proceeded to the Choice of a Commissioner in the Place of Jno Merryman who refused to act; when David Harris Esquire was unanimously chosen —— ————

BALTIMORE JANUARY 8th. 1789

Gentlemen / Sundry Freemen, naturalized Subjects and residents of this Town possessed of Every requisite required by Law and the Constitution of Maryland to qualify them as Voters having offered to poll at this Election— I am now to— demand those Votes may be entered on the Poll agreeable to Law and the Custom and usage heretofore observed, admitting to Every free Voter the liberty of Entering his objections thereto— This I humbly conceive to be the legal, Constitutional mode of Proceeding and so far as has come within my Knowledge, the Universal Plan persued (one Instance only Excepted)— Should you be of a different opinion On this Very important Question which will affect the Rights and Privileges of a Great Number of reputable Citizens and you think Proper to reject those Votes: I am then to request you will enter this demand in their Behalf on your proceedings—

I am respectfully Gentlemen Yr
Mo Ob. Sert. W SMITH L S
To the Comrs. of Balto Town

BALTIMORE 8 JANUARY 1789

We are of Opinion that a Foreigner naturalized agreeably to the act of Assembly "For Naturalization" passed July session 1779 is not entitled to Vote unless such foreigner *has resided* in Baltimore Town a Year after such Naturalization, altho such Foreigner may have *lived* in Baltimore Town above One year preceding the day of holding the Election and is Otherwise qualified to Vote—— DAN BOWLEY
WM. GOODWIN
DAVID HARRIS
SAML. CHASE

28th APRIL 1789—

The Commissioners met   Present
WM. GOODWIN   THOS. ELLIOT ⎫
DAN BOWLEY   PHILIP GRAYBELL ⎬ *Commrs.*
DAVID HARRIS   ⎭

The Commissioners being called on by Mr Jesse Hollingsworth to fix and Establish the East Corner of Wolf Street where it intersects Pitt Street Proceeded and fixed the said Corner by putting up a Stone having Examined Evidence and taken the deposition of Robert Long which is filed with the Comrs. Papers —— —— —— —— ——

Being also called on by Benjamin Griffith and Jeremiah Yellot to fix the south side of Fells Street they proceeded to examine Evidences respecting the same, and having taken the depositions of Bittingham Dickison and William Jacobs adjourned to Saturday for the purpose of Obtaining further Evidence to fix and Establish the same— The above depositions are filed with the Comrs. Papers— Wm Jacobs is appointed Clerk of the Point Market; at the Yearly Sallery of 20£ pr Annum   You do Swear that you will without favor affection or Partiality well and Truly execute the office of Clerk of the Point Market with Integrity and Honesty to the best of your Abilities: Wm. Jacobs was duly qualified before me the 30th of April 1787

L S   Thos. Elliot

1 JUNE 1790

The Commissioners met— Present   (The House of W Kellar)

Wm. Smith   Thomas Elliot ⎱
Dan Bowley   Philip Graybell ⎰ Comrs.

The Commissioners being called on by Archibald Steward to fix and ascertain the South East Corner of Fells Street and Bond street at their intersection, having Measured the Streets adjoining, And having ascertained the Same Do fix the said Corner Three feet North 54' East on the wall from the South West Corner of a Brick house now belonging to the said A. Steward and built by James Morgan—

JUNE 10th 1790—

The Commissioners met   Present

Jno. Moale   Wm Goodwin   David Harris ⎱
Wm Smith   Danl. Bowley   ⎰ Comrs.

The Commissioners proceeded to Elect a Commissioner in the Place of Rd Ridgely Esquire who had resigned, Samuel Chase Esqr. was appointed who qualified accordingly—

21 JUNE 1790—

The Commissioners met   Present

SAMUEL CHASE   THOMAS ELLIOT   DAN BOWLEY ⎱
DAVID HARRIS   PHILIP GRAYBELL   ⎰ Comrs.

The Commissioners being called upon by Mr. Daniel Grant
to Ascertain and fix the Corner of a Lott purchased by him
from George Lux upon light Lane as widened by Consent of
Parties the 16th. of July 1789 and having Measured the Grounds
and Streets adjoining Do find the North Side of the said Lott
purchased by Daniel Grant of George Lux to be twelve feet
south from the water Table of the South East Corner of the
Methodist meeting house on Light Street—

JULY 9th. 1790

The Commissioners met   Present   SAML. CHASE and
DAVID HARRIS but not making a Board they adjourned untill
called on — ————

JULY 10th. 1790—

The Commissioners met   Present

SAMUEL CHASE   DAVID HARRIS   ⎱
DANIEL BOWLEY   PHILIP GRAYBELL ⎰ Comrs.

The Commissioners then proceeded to the appointment of
an Inspector of flour when david Moor was unanimously appointed— Ordered that he have notice of the appointment
and that he qualify according to Law before the 20th Instant
and return a Certificate thereof— Ordered that the Several
Clerks of the Markets attend the Commissioners on friday
next to Settle their accounts—— Baltimore 12th July 1790
Personally appeared before me the Subscriber One of the
Justices of the Peace for Baltimore County David Moor first
being legally appointed Inspector of Flour for Baltimore Town
and took his affirmation of office according to Law —

L S   GEO: SALMON ——

JULY 15th. 1790—
(omitted)

The Commissioners met   Present

WM. GOODWIN   DAVID HARRIS ⎱
DAN BOWLEY   SAML. CHASE ⎰ Comrs.

The Commissioners proceeded to the Choice of a Commissioner in the place of Jno. Moale Esqur. who had resigned,

Philip Graybell Esqur. was unanimously chosen— Ordered that the Clerk give Notice of the appointment — (omitted)

19th. JULY 1790—

The Commissioners met   Present

SAML. CHASE   DAVID HARRIS } Comrs.
PHILIP GRAYBELL   DANL. BOWLEY }

The Commissioners being called on by Mr. Anthony Kemble to determine and fix the limits of Baltimore Street where he is about to build a New House so as to ascertain the front of his lott on the said Street: They find the distance to be Sixty Eight feet from the front of Nicholas Rogers store across the said Street the said Store of Mr. Rogers being two feet Back from the said Street ————————

The Commissioners met 25 JULY 1790

Present   SAML. CHASE   }
            DAVID HARRIS } Comrs.
            PHILIP GRAYBELL }

But there not being a sufficient Number to proceed to Business they adjourned untill the afternoon at 4 oClock ————

4th OCTOBER 1790

The Commissioners met   Present

WM SMITH   THOMAS ELLIOT   SAML CHASE } Comrs.
PHILIP GRAYBELL   WM. GOODWIN   }

The Commissioners proceeded to Elect a Commissioner in the Place of David Harris Esq. who had resigned and Wm. McLaughlin Esqr. was chosen ————————

Baltimore County to wit/ on the third day of January 1791 Personally appeared Archibald Campbell and Thomas Yates before me the Subscriber One of the Justices for the said County and made Oath on the Holy Evangel of Almighty God that they will faithfully and Honestly Execute the office and trust reposed in them as Auctioneers for Baltimore Town and that they will faithfully perform the Several duties required of them by Law without any Partiality fraud or deceit

L. S.   ARCHIBALD CAMPBELL
Sworn before   L. S.   THOMAS YATES
        WM RUSSELL

28th. FEBRUARY 1791

The Commissioners met   Present

Wm. Goodwin   Philip Graybell ⎱ Comrs—
Wm McLaughlin   Saml. Chase ⎰

The Commissioners having met at Mr. Grants agreeably to their advertisement in the Public Papers to consider of the Propriety of paving that Part of Pratt Street situate between Sharp Street and Hanover Street Do consent and approve that the Same shoud be paved agreeably to the Petition of the Inhabitants of the said Street; which is recorded among the Comrs. Papers———

28 MARCH 1791—

The Commissioners of Baltimore Town met by appointment of which Notice was given

Present Wm. Goodwin   Philip Graybell ⎱ Comrs.
Wm. McLaughlin Dan Bowley ⎰

The Intention of this Meeting being to Examine certain Charges and Allegations against David Moor the Present Inspector of flour (Mr. Moor being present) was called upon to hear the said Charges and Allegations which were read to him by the Clerk in the Order in which they are Numbered from No 1 to No 11 and which Said charges and the depositions in Support of them are filed with the Comrs. Papers— The Commissioners adjourn to Monday next in Order to give Mr. Moor an opportunity of Making his defence—against which day he is desired to be prepared — — —

N B. Mr. Moor's Examination was at Mr. Grants in Presence of a Number of respectable Gentlemen among whom were Messrs. Thomas Hollingsworth, James Gittings Senr. Jno. Stump and Brother, Wallis, Hart, Ogleby, John, Allen, Simpson, Jessop, Alexander, Legate—Mr. Legate was the Prosecutor— — —

4 APRIL 1791

The Commissioners met agreeably to Adjournment   Present

Dan Bowley   Philip Graybell ⎱ Comrs—
Wm Goodwin   Wm. McLaughlin ⎰

The Commissioners proceeded to hear and Examine Mr. Moor in Answer to the Charges brought against him as Inspector of Flour at the last Meeting and having heard his defence and duly considered all the Circumstances are Unanimously of Opinion that said Moor be continued in his office of Inspector of Flour for this Town — —

8th APRIL, 1791

The Commissioners Met   Present

WM GOODWIN   DAN BOWLEY   } Comrs—
WM MCLAUGHLIN   PHILIP GRAYBELL }

The Commissioners being called on by Harry Dorsey Gough Esquire and John McDonough to fix the North West Corner of St Pauls lane and Baltimore Street and to Establish the same by putting up a Stone at the Said Corner, Attended at the spot and saw the same set up, which they now fix and Establish as the Corner and Intersection of the said Lane and Baltimore Street agreeably to Mr. Goughs Petition in writing; which is filed with the Comrs. Papers

3 JUNE 1791—

The Commissioners met   Present

WM SMITH   WM MCLAUGHLIN } Comrs—
WM GOODWIN   DANIEL BOWLEY }

At the request of Captain Philip Graybell and Mr Peter Wyant the Commissioners proceeded to establish the Bounds of Captain Graybells Lott On Baltimore Street being part of the Original Town lott No 31. The begining of which they find to be exactly in the Center of his foundation Or Cellar Wall at the East End of his house now Erecting on the said Lott and it is fixed accordingly— — —

JULY 2nd 1791—

The Commissioners Met   Present

SAML. CHASE   WM. MCLAUGHLIN } Comrs—
WM. GOODWIN   DAN BOWLEY   }

The Commissioners being called on by Peter Wyant to Ascertain the Boundaries and lines of the Original Lotts No. 31 and 34 between Charles and Hanover Streets find that the North East Corner of a Brick Store built by John Ridgely Esquire and now belonging to Mrs Hudson is the Eastern Boundary and that the North West Corner of the Brick house wherein John Stark now keeps Tavern is the West boundary of the said Lotts on Baltimore Street and that there is a surplus of Twenty

Inches on the front of the said Lotts which they have divided
between the said Lotts and the Same is hereby Established by
them — — — — David Moor is appointed Inspector of flour
for Baltimore Town for this year, and is directed to qualify according to law — — —

7th JULY 1791

The Commissioners met   Present

SAML. CHASE   PHILIP GRAYBELL ⎱ Comrs—
WM McLAUGHLIN DANL. BOWLEY ⎰

The Commissioners having taken into Consideration the
present State of the Center Market, Ordered that the Clerk
of said Market procure an Estimate of the Expense of paving
the inside and footways of the upper Part of the said Market
from Baltimore to Second Street, and that he give Notice that
the Commissioners are ready and desirous to Employ Some
Person of Character to Compleat the said pavement ——

11th. JULY 1791—

The Commissioners Met

DANIEL BOWLEY   THOS. ELLIOT ⎱ Comrs.
Present— PHILIP GRAYBELL   WM. McLAUGHLIN ⎰

The Commissioners being called on by Mr. Christopher
Hughes to fix and Establish Lee Street at the intersection of
Hanover and Lee Streets, and also Hill street at the intersection of Hanover and Hill Streets proceeded and after Measuring the Same fixed them agreeably to Stones set up at the
said Corners Being also called on to fix and Establish the
Intersection of Forrest and Montgomery Streets proceeded to
Measure the Same but finding a disagreement in the Measurement of Seven feet and a half foot from a former Measurement and Survey adjourned to Monday the 25 Inst. to hear
Evidence and determine the Same— The Clerk is directed
to Settle his accounts and to call on the several Clerks of the
Markets to Come in by the 25th. of July and Settle theirs
respectively — — — — —

25th. JULY 1791

The Commissioners Met   Present

DANIEL BOWLEY   THOMAS ELLIOT ⎱
WM MCLAUGHLIN   PHILIP GRAYBELL ⎰ *Esqrs Comrs*

The Commissioners being called on by Mr. Christopher Hughes, John Mickle and John McDonough to Ascertain and fix the South East Corner of Montgomery and Forrest Streets attended at the spot and after Taking the depositions of John Elder Gist and Solomon Himes fixed the said Corner at the distance of forty One feet three Inches East on Montgomery Street from a log house built by the said Solomon Himes and placed a Stone there as a Boundary for the Same. Gist's deposition filed with Comrs. Papers— — —

25 JULY 1791—

The Commissioners Met

Present   DANIEL BOWLEY   THOMAS ELLIOT ⎱
          PHILIP GRAYBELL   WM MCLAUGHLIN ⎰ *Comrs.*

The Clerk of the Commissioners is requested to give Public Notice that the Comrs. of Baltimore Town will meet on Monday the 15th. day of August Next to consider the Propriety of paving that part of Baltimore Street between Liberty and Howard Streets and of that part of Charles Street between Pratt and New Church Streets— The Commissioners will also on that day appoint a Measurer of Grain for the Town of Baltimore— Resolved that One hundred Dollars arrising from the fines on flour &c be paid to Captain Thomas Johnson Messrs David Plunket and Wm. McCreery for the Purpose of putting a New Roof on the Point Market— — The Clerk of the Commissoners who was called on at the last Meeting to settle his accounts, produced the same and on a settlement after Examination there appeared a Balance in favor of him of Sixty four Pounds Three Shillings and four Pence.— — —

Baltimore County to wit   August 1st. 1791 Personally appeared before the Subscriber One of the Justices of Oyer and Terminer David Moor and took his affirmation of Office as inspector of flour for the Port of Baltimore

before JAMES CALHOUN—L S—

17th. AUGUST 1791—

The Commissioners of Baltimore Town met

	SAML. CHASE	PHILIP GRAYBELL	
Present	DANL. BOWLEY	WM. GOODWIN	*Comrs.*— —
	THOMAS ELLIOT		

The Commissioners of Baltimore Town having considered the Propriety of paving that part of Baltimore Street between Liberty and Howard Streets and of that part of Charles Street between Pratt and Chatham Streets Do approve that the same be paved and Order that the special Commissioners have Notice accordingly— — The Commissioners of Baltimore Town resolve to appoint two Persons to be Measurer of all Grain and flax Seed brought by land or Water and offered for sale and Salt Sold in Baltimore Town for One year to commence On the first day of September Next— The Commissioners having qualified agreeably to act of Assembly 1771 ch. 20 proceeded to appoint Two Persons to be Measurers of Grain for the Town of Baltimore when Benjamin Dashiell and Charles Wells were appointed— Ordered that Daniel Bowley pay to the Gentlemen appointed to repair the Point Market the Sum of One hundred Dollars of the Money in his hands arrising from the Penalties on Condemned flour agreeably to the Orders of the Board Ordered that the Clerk of the Commissioners procure a Mahogany Chest to contain the records and the Platts of the Town with two Keys to the lock at least for the use of the Commissioners— — —

25th DAY AUGUST 1791

The Commissioners met

	WM. SMITH	SAML. CHASE	
Present	PHILIP GRAYBELL	WM MCLAUGHLIN	*Comrs* —
	THOMAS ELLIOT	DAN BOWLEY	

Mr. Nathaniel Smith Inspector of Salted Provision having informed the Comrs. that Several Persons had exported from out of Patapsco River Some Barrells of fish not Examined and branded as the act of assembly of November session 1786 C 17 Sec 13 requires Ordered that Richard Moale Clerk of this Board procure a warrant in the Name of the Commissioners for the Penalty of 50 s Currency Money for Every Barrell so

exported at any Time within One year before the Time of
Obtaining such warrant and that he attend Some Justice of the
Peace on the hearing of the said warrant and that he be allowed
Ten pr. Cent on the Money recovered— Mr. Nathaniel Smith
having also informed this Board that Several Persons had
Purchased and that Others had offered for sale and in Some
Instances sold within this Town and its Prescincts   Some Barrells of fish not Examined and branded as the act of Assembly of Novr. Session 1790. ch. 31. Sect. 6 requires, Ordered
that the said Nathaniel Smith apply to the attorney General
and inform him of the Violation of the said Law and that the
said Nathaniel Smith lay the same before the Next Grand
Jury for Baltimore County — — The Board agree that application be made to the legislature at their Next session to inflict
a Certain Penalty on Every Person who Shall purchase or Sell
or offer to sell within this Town or its Prescincts any Salted
Provisions not Examined and branded agreeably to the directions of the act of November Session 1786 and that the
Clerk prepare a Petition for this Purpose — — — — —

24 NOVEMBER 1791—

The Commissioners met

	SAML. CHASE	WM GOODWIN	
Present	PHILIP GRAYBELL		Comrs —
	WM McLAUGHLIN	THOMAS ELLIOT	

David Moor the Inspector of Flour for Baltimore Town having passed a quantity of Flour as Common fine the property of
Thomas Wilson which upon the review of three Persons appointed by a Magistrate to inspect the Same was determined
by them to be Superfine; and the said Moor refusing to pass
the said Flower as such And a Complaint being lodged
against him by the said Wilson: He appeared to answer the
Same, but the Commissioners having Examined the Law, and
finding they have no power by the said Law to give redress in
Such Cases dismissed the Complaint   Mr. John Hammond
having produced his account Amounting to Six pounds sixteen
Shillings and Ten Pence ½ Against the Commissioners for
Sand furnished the Marsh Market, the Commis. after
having examined the Same Ordered it to be paid on the first
day of May 1792 — — —

12th MARCH 1792

The Commissioners met ——

Present   Wm McLaughlin   Wm. Goodwin ⎱ Comrs—
           Philip Graybell   Dan Bowley ⎰

The Commissioners being called upon by Mr. William Gouldsmith to fix his lot of Ground on the Corner of Gay and Harrison Streets and having Measured the Same,—have Established the Corner of the said Lott at the intersection of the
Said Two Streets to be fifty feet Easterly in a Perpendicular
line from the West side of Gay street taking the front of
Saml Messersmiths house for the said West side and to front
on Gay street thirty three feet and a half —— —— ——

MARCH 22nd 1792

The Commissioners Met   Present

   Saml. Chase   Daniel Bowley ⎱
   Wm Goodwin   Wm McLaughlin ⎰ Comrs—
   Philip Graybell   Thomas Elliot ⎰

The Commissioners of Baltimore Town being called on by
Mr. Richardson Stewart and John Hammond to fix and ascertain the Corner of Connawager Street and a Ten feet alley
leading from Market Street to Charles Street, after having
Measured the lotts and streets Contigeous to the Same
fixed the said Corner and put down a Stone Marked R S. as a
Boundary for the Same at the intersection of the said Street
and Alley and On the West said of the Alley — —

3d. MAY 1792   A. M—

The Commissioners met —— Present

   Wm. Smith   Wm McLaughlin ⎱ Comrs.—
   Philip Graybell   Thomas Elliot ⎰

The South East Corner of the Square bounding on Water
Street and Frederick Street Established by begining at the
South East Corner of the Square bounding On Water Street
and Gay street and at the Corner of the Brick house Owned by
the late Mr. John Sterett and runing thence bounding on the
North side of Water Street Easterly two hundred and thirty
One feet to a Stone standing Northerly Forty Nine feet and a
half from the North East Corner of the house built by Mr.
William Buchanan and at present Owned by Mr. John O'Don-
nell — —

3d MAY 1792   P M—

The Commissioners met   Present

WM SMITH   WM MCLAUGHLIN ⎫
PHILIP GRAYBELL   THOS ELLIOT   ⎬ *Comrs.*—
                                   ⎭

The Commissioners being called on by General Williams to ascertain the South East Corner at the intersection of Water and Frederick streets having Measured the Streets and the lotts adjoining the Same begining at a Brick House Owned by the heirs of Mr John Sterett deceased fixed and Established the said Corner two hundred and thirty One feet Easterly from the said John Steretts Brick house and forty nine feet northerly from a Brick house built by Mr. William Buchanan and Owned by John O Donell and put down a stone at the intersection aforesaid as a Boundary for the Same — —

The Port Wardens and Special Commissioners having produced a Bond required by Act of assembly respecting the Annual Lottery for the Town of Baltimore for the approbation of the Commissioners of the Town the same being Examined was approved by them — — ———

15 MAY 1792

The Commissioners Met — Present

WILLIAM GOODWIN   PHILIP GRAYBELL ⎫
THOMAS ELLIOT   DAN BOWLEY   ⎬ *Comrs.*—
                                  ⎭

The Commissioners being called by John Weaver to ascertain the Northwest side of Fells Street in Order to fix the front of his Lott after Measuring the said Street have determined the line of the said North West side thereof to be from the front of John Bernards House to the Angle or Corner of a House built by George Wells at the Intersection of Thames and Fells Streets —

29th MAY 1792

The Commissioners   Met

          WILLIAM SMITH   PHILIP GRAYBELL ⎫
Present   WM. MCLAUGHLIN THOMAS ELLIOT   ⎬ *Comrs.*—
                                           ⎭

The Commissioners being called on by John Hammond and Mr John ODonnell to pay off their respective accounts for paving the Center Market and Materials furnished for paving the same having examined the said accounts and passed them for payment at former Meeting: Ordered their Clerk to pay the Same and take receipts therefor— — Ordered that the Clerk make out the Number of days Wm Smith Wm. McLaughlin and Philip Graybell Esquires attended this board as Commissioners and to pay them respectively for the Same— Ordered that David Moor the Inspector of flour render an Account of what Money he has received for fines and forfeitures Since his last Settlement and that the same may be paid Over to the Order of the Commissioners of Baltimore Town— Ordered that James Long settle his accounts and pay Over the Balance to the Clerk of the Commissioners— Resolved that the Commissioners of Baltimore Town will meet at the Court House on the first Monday in July Next at Ten oClock and On Every first Monday at the Same hour in Every Month thereafter throughout the year — — —

Ordered that the Clerk give Notice in the public Papers that the Commsrs of Baltmore Town will meet at the Court House on the first Monday in July next at Ten oClock and On the first Monday in Every Month at the Same hour and Place thereafter throughout the year ——

2 JULY 1792

The Commissioners met Agreeably to Notice,

Present
WM SMITH WILLIAM McLAUGHLIN ⎫
PHILIP GRAYBELL THOMAS ELLIOT ⎬ Comrs.
⎭

The Commissioners of Baltimore Town having first taken the Oath directed by the Act of Assembly passed in 1781. Ch. 12. proceeded to the appointment of an Inspector of Flour for the Town and port of Baltimore when David Moor the late Inspector of Flour was appointed, who qualified by affirmation before Thomas Elliot Esquire agreeably to the directions of the aforesaid Act and returned his Certificate of the Same to the Clerk of the Commissioners of Baltimore Town— — David Moor being called on by the Clerk as directed at the last Meeting to Settle his Accounts and to pay over the Balance to the Commissioners produced the Same and there appearing to be a Balance of forty Seven pounds thirteen Shillings received by him for fines and forfeitures, paid the Amount Over to them for the use of Baltimore Town— I hereby Certify that David Moor took the affirmation of office as Inspector of flour for the Port and Town of Baltimore before me agreeably to the directions contained in the Act of assembly November Session 1781—

Baltimore July 2nd, 1792. — — THOMAS ELLIOT   L S

27th. JULY 1792

The Commissioners Met

Present   WM. GOODWIN   WM. MCLAUGHLIN ⎫
          DAN BOWLEY   PHILIP GRAYBELL ⎬ Comrs.
          THOMAS ELLIOT   ⎭

The Commissioners of Baltimore Town being called on by Mr. James Long to fix and ascertain the South West Corner of lott Number 14 at the intersection of front and Lowe Streets after having Examined Mr. Peter Litzinger on Oath and having taken his deposition which is here recorded and having also Measured the Streets and Lotts adjoining and contigueous thereto adjourned untill the first day of August Next at which time a Stone is to be put down at the intersection aforesaid as a Boundary for the Corner of Lott Number 14 at the intersection aforesaid at the Corner of Long's Brick house

JULY 31st. 1792

The Commissioners met

Present   PHILIP GRAYBELL ⎫
          THOMAS ELLIOT ⎬ Comrs —
          WM MCLAUGHLIN ⎭

The commissioners being called to fix and ascertain the South West Corner of Baltimore Street at the intersection of Baltimore and Howard Streets coud not proceed to fix and Establish the Same there not being Sufficient Members of their Board Present to execute the Same — — —

6th. AUGUST 1792.

The Commissioners Met

Present   PHILIP GRAYBELL   THOMAS ELLIOT ⎫ Comrs.
          WM. MCLAUGHLIN   DAN BOWLEY ⎬

The Commissioners having Met agreeably to their adjournment of the 2nd. July 1792 at James Longs to fix and Ascertain the Corner of Lott Number 14 at the Intersection of lowe and front Streets, having Measured the Streets and Lotts adjoining the Same at a former Meeting fixed the said Corner at the Intersection aforesaid by putting down a Stone marked on the East side thereof with the Letters L S—and on the West side of the said Stone with the Number 14— — — The Commissioners at their last Meeting having to confirm them in their Judgment respecting the fixing and ascertaining the said Corner at the intersection aforesaid taken the deposition of a Certain Peter Litzinger which is filed with the Commissioners Papers No. 42— The Commissioners having also at a former Meeting Measured from the Corner of Lowe and front Streets on the North side of front Street to a Locust Post standing at the Begining of Lott No 13. and having the Same Proof that the said Post is the Begining of the said Lott No 13 fixed the Same as the Begining of the said Lott No 13 by putting down a Stone Marked on the East side thereof with the No. 13 and on the west side of the same with the Number 14 as the Begining of the said Lott No 13——

5 SEPTEMBER 1792

The Commissioners Met

WILLIAM GOODWIN   THOMAS ELLIOT ⎫
Present PHILIP GRAYBELL   WM MCLAUGHLIN ⎭ *Comrs —*

The Commissioners being called on by Mr. Lewis Pascault to Establish the Corner of his Lott at the Intersection of Baltimore and Howard Streets and lying and bounding on the West side of Howard Street and South side of Baltimore Street Do fix the Same at the distance of Eighty Two feet one Inch and One half of an Inch from a Wooden Building erected by Daniel Lamott and now in possession of Peter Forney —— —— ——

28th. September 1792

At a Meeting of the Commissioners the following Members attended

SAMUEL CHASE   THOMAS ELLIOT ⎫
WM SMITH   PHILIP GRAYBELL ⎭ *Comrs* ——

Resolved that the Sallery of the Clerk of the Center Market be and continue the Sum of Thirty Pounds per Annum—and that the Sallery of the Clerks of the Point and Hill Markets be the Sum of Fifteen Pounds Each per Annum— The Com-

missioners appoint James Long Clerk of the Center Market—
Septimus Noel Clerk of the Hill Market and William Jacobs
Clerk of the Point Market— Resolved the different Clerks
of the Several Markets in Baltimore Town render a regular account for the ensuing year of All Monies received for Weighing Meat and Other things and for all Seizures made by them
— and that the several Clerks for the Said Markets be allowed
50 pr Cent on all Monies received by them on account of
weighing and for all Seizures made by them—— —— — —

5th. NOVEMBER 1792.

The Commissioners met   Present

SAML. CHASE   WM. SMITH   WM. McLAUGHLIN ⎫
PHILIP GRAYBELL THOMAS ELLIOT   ⎬ Comrs—
                                             ⎭

The Commissioners of Baltimore Town having qualified
agreeably to the act of Assembly passed in November Session
1771. Chap. 20 appointed John Gottro and Paul Beshean Corders of Wood for Baltimore Town and Peter Weary Corder of
Wood for Fells Point— Having also qualified by taking the
Oath prescribed by the Act of Assembly passed November
Session 1771. Cha: 20 the Commissioners appointed Richard
Boulding to be the Weigher of all hay brought by land or
water for sale to Baltimore Town for the Ensuing year—
Ordered that the Wood Corders and Hay Weighers qualify
according to the aforesaid Act— — — —

Philip Graybell Esquire is appointed to Examine the Hay
Scales and Weights and to See that they are in proper Order—

17 NOVEMBER 1792

The Commissioners Met   Present

WM SMITH   PHILIP GRAYBELL ⎫
THOMAS ELLIOT   WM McLAUGHLIN   ⎬ Comrs. —
                                   ⎭

Paul Beshean heretofore appointed Wood Corder for Baltimore Town at a former Meeting having refused to Serve;
The Commissioners appoint George Rhotrock Wood Corder
in his Place and Order the Clerk to give him Notice of his
appointment that he may qualify accordingly— Resolved
that Richard Moale Clerk to the Commissioners have and

receive Seven Shillings and Six pence for Each and Every day he has and shall attend this Board at Elections for Baltimore Town—and that the same be allowed him in his Account with the Commissioners of Baltimore Town—— —— ——

I hereby Certify that George Rothrock appeared before me the Subscriber a Justice of the Peace for Baltimore County and took the Oath prescribed by the act of Assembly faithfully to Execute the office of Wood Corder for Baltimore Town without favor, affection or Partiality—   Sworn before

THOMAS ELLIOT—L S—

Balto. November 26. 1792.

Baltimore County to wit   March 12 1793 I do hereby certify that Richard Bouldin this day took the Oath of Weigher of hay for Baltimore Town before me

Signed—THOMAS ELLIOT

And Likewise declared his belief in the Christian Relegion

Signed RICHARD BOULDIN

16th. MARCH 1793

The Commissioners Met   Present

| SAML. CHASE | PHILIP GRAYBELL | } Comrs—— |
| WM McLAUGHLIN | WM GOODWIN | |

The Commissioners of Baltimore Town having Met to appoint an Inspector of Salted Provisions for the Town of Baltimore Mr. Nathaniel Smith was Appointed to that office and took the Oath of office before Wm. McLaughlin Esqr. Wm. Guffey was appointed Deputy Inspector of Salted Provisions for the Town by Mr Nathaniel Smith with the consent and approbation of the Commissioners of the said Town— — — —

APRIL 1st, 1793

The Commissioners met   Present

| WM. SMITH | WILLIAM GOODWIN | } Comrs.—— |
| PHILIP GRAYBELL | WM McLAUGHLIN | |

The Commissioners being called On by Jacob Miller to fix and Ascertain the West side of Jones's Street, began to Measure from the North West Corner of a Brick house built by John Brown and William Wilson and now Owned by Colo

Barber of Virginia standing at the End of the first line of
Lott No 1 on Jones's Street and On the west side of the said
Street and having Measured along the Same fixed the West
side of said street at the Bend in the Lott No. 3 by putting
down a Stone, which they Now Establish as the Boundary of
the West side of the said Street—and having cited from the
said Bend when they placed the aforesaid Stone to the Brick
Store owned by James Edwards at the Intersection of Bridge
and Jones's Streets Established the said Brick Store as the
West side of the said Street— — —

2nd APRIL 1793.

The Commissioners met agreeably to adjournment

Present
WM. SMITH   WM. GOODWIN   } Comrs—
PHILIP GRAYBELL   WM McLAUGHLIN }

The Commissioners at the request of Mr. Jas Sommerville
met at the Intersection of North Lane and Baltimore Street
and Established the East Corner of North Lane on Baltimore
Street at the distance of Sixteen feet and One half of a foot
from the house now occupied by James Calhoun Esquire They
also fix North Lane on the West side thereof at a Stake Now
set down on the South Side of Jones's Falls close by the Edge
of the Falls — ———

The Commissioners at the request of Messrs. Thomas Mc-
Eldery and James Dale also fix the West side of the Street
now called Hollidays street at the distance of Sixty five feet
from the West Corner of a Brick house Standing on Market
Street and built by Mark Alexander, which house is now
occupied by Robert Walsh— Adjourned untill Tuesday 9th.
Inst. 3 oClock P M

16 JUNE 1793

The Commissioners met   Present

WM SMITH   WM. McLAUGHLIN } Comrs—
WM. GOODWIN   PHILIP GRAYBELL }

The Commissioners met on the application of Mr. Hillen to
appoint One Other Weigher of Hay for Baltimore Town, but
the act of Assembly directing the appointment to be made
between the first and last days of November they declined
appointing untill November Next — — — —

18. JUNE 1793.—

At the Instance of Alexander Lawson The Commissioners of Baltimore Town met On the Premises to ascertain the South West Corner of Back Street— —

	SAMUEL CHASE	WM. GOODWIN	
Present	WM SMITH	PHILIP GRAYBELL	}Comrs —
	THOMAS ELLIOT	WM McLAUGHLIN	

The Commissioners with the assistance of Mr. Cornelius Howard the Surveyor having run the lines in two directions do fix and establish the said South west Corner of Back Street as follows to wit. Run'g N. 41. ¼ East from the North East Corner of the Lutheran Parsonage House 100 feet to the south west Corner of Back Street also from the south side of East lane run Northerly 354½ feet to the aforesaid South West Corner of Back Street which fixes the Corner Exactly — —

13th JULY 1793—

The Commissioners met to appoint an Inspector of flour for the Ensuing year—

	SAML. CHASE	PHILIP GRAYBELL	}Comrs—
Present	THOMAS ELLIOT	WM. McLAUGHLIN	

The Commissioners having qualified agreeably to the act of Assembly passed at November Session 1781. ch. 12 appointed David Moor to be Inspector of flour for the Town and Port of Baltimore for the Ensuing year the said David Moor qualified in the Presence of the Commissioners before Thomas Elliot Esquire. — —

12th. JULY 1793

The Commissioners Met

	WM SMITH	THOMAS ELLIOT	}Comrs —
Present	PHILIP GRAYBELL	WM. GOODWIN	

The Commissioners with the Consent of the Owners and proprietors of that part of the land situate on East lane conveyed by a Certain Alexander Lawson to John Smith and Others on the 21st. of October 1765 did Condemn, adjudge and declare the ground mentioned and covenanted to be kept open as a part of East lane, as and for one of the public Streets of Baltimore Town by the Name of East Street, and Entitled

to all the Privileges and Subject to the Charges of the Other
Streets of the said Town That is to say—all that Space of
ground lying between the Original additional Part (Mentioned in the said Deed) and East lane being of the Breadth
of Sixteen feet and one half of a foot and Extending of
an Equal Width from the Corner of North lane bounding
on East Street or East lane to Calvert Street—of which said
Condemnation and adjudication the said Commissioners have
caused this record to be made among their proceedings—

30th. OCTOBER 1793—

The Commissioners of Baltimore Town in Consequence of
the Death of Major Nathaniel Smith the late Inspector of
Salted Provisions for the said Town met at the Court house
for the purpose of choosing an Inspector in his Place

	SAML. CHASE	PHILIP GRAYBELL	
Present	WM SMITH	WM. McLAUGHLIN	Comrs—
	WM. GOODWIN	DAN BOWLEY and	
		THOMAS ELLIOT ESQRS.	

The Commissioners of Baltimore Town after taking the
Oath required by the Act of Assembly passed November Session 1786 entitled an Act for the Inspection of Salted provisions
proceeded to nominate and appoint a Person to be inspector
of Salted Beef, Pork and fish in Barrells within the said Town
of Baltimore for the residue of the Present year and in the
place of Major Nathaniel Smith deceased and made choice of
Adam Jemason to be inspector of Salted Provisions aforesaid
for the residue of the present year agreeably to the act of
Assembly in Such Case made & provided— It was agreed by
the Commissioners that the Person appointed Inspector of
Salted Provisions for Baltimore Town must have a Majority
of the Votes of the Commissioners of the said Town— Ordered
that the Clerk give Notice of the appointment and that Adam
Jemason do qualify agreeably to the act of Assembly directing
the Same, which was accordingly done and the said qualification is filed with the Commissioners Papers No. 57— —

NOVEMBER 4th. 1793.—

The Commissioners Met

Daniel Bowley	Thomas Elliot	}
Present Philip Graybell	Wm. McLaughlin	Comrs —

The Commissioners upon the application of Adam Jemason the Inspector of Salted Provisions approve of the appointment of William Guffey as his deputy Inspector of Salted Provisions for Baltimore Town and direct the said William Guffey to qualify as Such agreeably to the Act of Assembly directing the same which was accordingly done, and his qualification filed among the Commissioners Papers No 59——

They also appoint Abraham Norris as Weigher of hay for Baltimore Town at the Scales on Machine of Solomon Hillen at the East End of the said Town and direct him to qualify agreeably to the directions of the act of Assembly directing the Same, which was done and his qualification filed among the Comrs. Papers No 60—

16th. NOVEMBER 1793.—

The Commissioners met

Wm. Smith	Philip Graybell	}
Present Wm. McLaughlin	Thomas Elliot	Comrs —

The Commissioners of Baltimore Town being called on by Thomas Coulston to fix and ascertain the south East Corner of Holliday Street continued and East street at their Intersection, having Measured the Lotts and Streets thereto adjoining declare the South East Corner of a Brick warehouse now building for James Dale to be the south East Corner of the said streets at their Intersection and Established the Same accordingly— Thomas McEldery Esquire having offered to lend the Commissioners of Baltimore Town One hundred Pounds free and Clear of Interest untill paid for the Purpose of filling up and paving the Lower End of the Center Market house Resolved that the Commissioners of Baltimore Town do accept of the Same for the purposes aforesaid: and that Richard Moale have full Powers to contract with any Person to perform the same under the immediate Inspection of James Long the Clerk of the said Market—

17 FEBRUARY 1794.

The Commissioners of Baltimore Town   Met

	SAMUEL CHASE	DANIEL BOWLEY	
Present WM. GOODWIN	THOMAS ELLIOT	} Comrs —
	PHILIP GRAYBELL	WM. MCLAUGHLIN	

The Commissioners being called on by Thomas McEldery
and Cumberland Dugan to consider the propriety of Granting
the following application to wit

To the Commissioners of Baltimore Town

GENTLEMEN

We the Subscribers request your Permis-
sion for making a Canal and Wharf at our Expense in the
Market Space from the south side of Prat Street to the Channel or Warden's Line the canal to be Eighty feet wide and
the Streets on Each side the Same to be thirty five feet wide;
the Said Canal, Wharf and Streets to be made public for the
use of the Inhabitants under the Laws and regulations of your
Board and the whole of the same to be relinquished up to the
Commissioners whenever the Same or any Part thereof may
be Wanted for Market houses — —

Your Mo. Ob. Ser vts.

CUMBERLAND DUGAN

Baltimore 10th. Feby 1794 Signed THOMAS MCELDERY

The Commissioners of Baltimore Town having considered
the above application have no objection to Messrs. Thomas
McEldery and Cumberland Dugan filling up the Space of
150 feet wide on a line with the present Market Space from
Water Street as far as a line drawn from the south side of
Prat Street shall intersect or Cross the said Space and after
filling up the said space the Commissioners have no Objection
to their Making a Canal from the said line of Intersection to
the Channel of 60 feet wide with wharves and a street on Each
side of said Canal of forty five feet wide, but with this Express declaration that the Privilege of filling up said Canal
and of the whole space of 150 feet wide be fully reserved to the
said Commissioners and their Successors for the use of the
said Town as granted by the act of Assembly of November

Session 1784 C 62 entitled an Act for establishing new Markets &c &c and also on this Express condition that the said Canal, wharves and Streets on Each side of the said Canal be a Common high way and free for the Public use, and Subject to such regulations as the Commissioners and their Successors shall from time to Time establish; and On this further Express Condition that the said McEldery and Dugan Extend Pratt Street thro their two Lotts of Ground on Each side of the said Market Space and leave Pratt Street of the Width of 60 feet thro their Said Lotts forever as a Street for the use of the Public forever thereafter— —

The Commissioners having also considered the application of the Proprietors of the Lotts on an Alley called Ruxtons Alley Extending East from Charles Street to light lane to have the same condemned as a Public high way for the use of Baltimore Town— As also the application of the Proprietors of the Lotts on Wilkes's Lane Extending West from St. Pauls Lane to Charles Street praying a Condemnation of the Same for the use of the said Town Do hereby condemn the said Lane and Alley as a Public high way for the use of Baltimore Town forever— The application of the Proprietors of Lotts on Wilkes Lane and also that of Ruxton's alley are filed among the Comrs. Papers Nos. 63. 64

19th. MARCH 1794

The Commissioners Met   Present

| Wm. Goodwin | Philip Graybell | } Comrs — |
| Thomas Elliot | Wm. McLaughlin | |

The Commissioners having Met to appoint an Inspector of Salted Provisions for Baltimore Town for the year Ensuing appointed Mr Adam Jemason to that office who is directed to qualify agreeably to the directions of the act of assembly requiring the same which is accordingly done and filed with the Comrs. Papers No 66 The Commissioners being first qualified Agreeably to the act of Assembly before the appointment— Wm. Guffey being appointed Deputy Inspector of Salted Provisions for the said Town by Adam Jemason, the Commissioners do approve of the said appointment and direct William Guffey to qualify accordingly which he did, and the Same is filed with the Commissioners Papers No 67 — —

28th. APRIL 1794

The Commissiones Met

Present   SAMUEL CHASE   PHILIP GRAYBELL ⎱ _Comrs—_
        THOMAS ELLIOT   WM McLAUGHLIN ⎰

The Commissioners being called on by George Sears to fix
and Establish the South West Corner of Howard and Fayette
Streets having Measured the Same Do ascertain the Same to
be at a Stake to be set up at the distance of Sixty Six feet three
Inches on a Straight Line drawn with Howard Street and
Parallel thereto from the Corner of William Winchesters
Brick house which he now lives in on the West side of How-
ard's Street

JUNE 2nd 1794

The Commissioners met

  WM SMITH   WM. GOODWIN ⎱ _Comrs —_
  THOMAS ELLIOT   PHILIP GRAYBELL ⎰

The Commissioners being called on by Charles Torrence
to ascertain and fix the Corner of Wapping and front Streets
at their intersection having Measured the said Streets and the
Lotts adjoining Do fix the same by putting down a Stone at the
south West Corner of the said Streets which they Now declare
and fix as the Corner of the said Streets at their Intersection —

2nd. JUNE 1794

The Commissioners met

  W SMITH   WM GOODWIN ⎱ _Comrs —_
  PHILIP GRAYBELL THOMAS ELLIOT ⎰

The Commissioners having met at the house of Captain
Thomas Elliot for the purpose of appointing a Clerk of the
Hanover Market in the Place of Mr. Septimus Noel deceased,
proceeded to the appointment when Levallin Barry was Elected,
and is directed to give Bond with Two sufficient Securities and
to take the Oath of office as required by the act of Assembly
directing the Same; which he accordingly did, and which are
filed with the Commissioners Papers Numbers 71. and 72— —

Resolved that the Stall rents of the Center Market commenc-
ing the 28th of April 1795 and Ending the 28th. of April 1795
be raised to the Sum of Ten Dollars Each pr Annum— And
that any Butcher who shall Erect a stall in the lower part of

the Center Market house shall have the same with all the Priviledges annexed to the Stalls in the upper Part of the said Market free and Clear of all Rent whatsoever for One Year and shall have the said stall for the year Ensuing at the rent or Sum of four Dollars— Ordered that James Long the Clerk of the Center Market compleat the Two first stalls in the lower Part of the said Market and be impowered by us to rent the Same for the Sum of Three Pounds Each pr. Annum— Resolved that any Person renting a stall in any Part of the said Market who shall neglect or refuse to pay all Arrearages due upon the Same for the space of Thirty days next after Demand made shall forfeit the said Stall and the Clerk of the said Market is hereby empowered and directed to rent the Same to any Person applying for the Same— Resolved that James Long the Clerk of the said Market be impowered and he is hereby by us directed to prevent all Persons from Selling or offering for sale any fish in the space called Second Street between the upper and lower End of the said Market and he is requested to direct any Person offering fish for sale in the space aforesaid to the lower End of the Market square where they may be accomodated.

12 JULY 1794

The Commissioners Met   Present

WM. SMITH   WM. GOODWIN   ⎫
THOMAS ELLIOT   PHILIP GRAYBELL   ⎬ Comrs —
          SAMUEL CHASE   ⎭

The Commissioners of Baltimore Town having met to appoint an Inspector of flour for the Town of Baltimore proceeded to the appointment when David Moor was unanimously appointed Inspector of flour for the said Town, who being present qualified according to the act of Assembly requiring the Same before Thomas Elliot Esqr.

27th. NOVEMBER 1794—

The Commissioners met   Present

PHILIP GRAYBELL   THOMAS ELLIOT   ⎫ Comrs —
WM. GOODWIN   WM McLAUGHLIN   ⎭

The Commissioners of Baltimore Town having met at John Starks Tavern agreeably To an advertisement in the Public Papers for the purpose of appointing Measurers of Grain,

Wood-Corders and hay weighers for Baltimore Town for the
year ensuing agreeably to the act of Assembly directing the
same proceeded to the Several appointments when Charles
Wells was appointed Measurer of Grain for Baltimore Town
and Benjamin Dashiell Measurer of Grain for that Part of
Baltimore Town called fells Point; John Gottro is appointed
wood-Corder for that Part of Baltimore Town west of Ellicots
Dock in a Line North with the East side of Light Street—
Robert Thornburgh Wood-Corder of that Part of Baltimore
Town between Ellicots Dock and Prestmans wharf inclusive—
Charles Merriken wood-Corder of that Part of Baltimore
Town between Prestman's wharf and the west side of Gay
Street— Godfry Hartung Wood-Corder of that part of Balti-
more Town from the East Side of Gay Street to the Wind
Mill Point and Peter Weary wood-Corder for that part of
Baltimore Town lying to the Southward and Eastward of the
said Wind Mill Point— Abraham Norris and Richard
Bouldin are appointed Weighers of hay for Baltimore Town
for the Ensuing year— The several officers are ordered
to file their Respective Oaths of office agreeably to the act of
Assembly under which they are appointed; which was done
accordingly by John Gottro, Robert Thornburgh, Charles Merriken, Godfry Hartung and Peter Weary Wood Corders and
by Richard Bouldin Hay Weighers which said Several Oaths
of office are filed with the Commissioners Papers Nos. 76.
77. 78. 79. 80. 81— The Petition of Sundry Inhabitants of
Baltimore Town praying that the Name of Smock alley
may be changed to that of Loyds Lane Resolved that the
Same is hereby Granted and the said Alley is hereafter to be
called and known *only* by the Name of Loyd's Lane for Ever
hereafter— The petition is filed among the Commissioners
Papers No 89 — — — — — — — — — —

19. MARCH 1795.

The Commissioners met   Present

SAMUEL CHASE   WM SMITH   ⎫
WM GOODWIN   THOMAS ELLIOT ⎬*Comrs* —
            PHILIP GRAYBELL.   ⎭

The Commissioners of Baltimore Town proceeded to fill
up the Vacancy in their Board occasioned by the Death of
William McLaughlin Esquire when David McMechen Esquire

was duly Elected who qualified himself by taking the Oath of Allegiance prescribed in the Constitution and Oath of office that he woud well and faithfully Execute the office and Duty of a Commissioner of Baltimore Town according to the best of his understanding and Judgment— The Commissioners displace Robert Thornburgh one of the Wood Corders Abraham Norris one of the Hay Weighers and will appoint Other Persons to Supply their Places on Wednesday Next— The Commissioners adjourned untill Saturday the 21st. Instant when they will appoint an Inspector of Salted Provisions for the said Town— ————

20th. MARCH 1795.

The Commissioners of Baltimore Town   Met

SAML. CHASE	PHILIP GRAYBELL
WM SMITH	
WM GOODWIN	DAVID MCMECHEN

} Comrs —

The Commissioners having met to consider whether they have the Power under the act of Assembly passed at November Session 1786. Ch. 17 to appoint an Inspector of Salted Provisions for the Town of Baltimore on this day are of Opinion they have not the Power— — — ————

25th. MARCH 1795.

The Commissioners Met   Present

SAMUEL CHASE
WM GOODWIN   } Comrs —
PHILIP GRAYBELL

But there not being sufficient Number of Members present to make a board for Business, they adjourned to the Next Meeting — — — — ———

10th. April 1795.

The Commissioners met at the house of Samuel Chase Esquire

Present SAML. CHASE   PHILIP GRAYBELL } Comrs —
    WM. GOODWIN   DAVID MCMECHEN

A Majority of the Proprietors of the Ground made and Extended into the Bason of the North West Branch of Patapsco River below Water Street and between a lane called by the Name of Franklin Lane and 83 feet East of a Street called by the Name of South Street having applied to this Board to direct the said Ground to be Surveyed &c It is ordered by the Commissioners that the said Ground and Space above described be Surveyed and laid out into Streets Lanes Lotts and Allyes and a Correct Platt and Certificate thereof be made and delivered to the Clerk of the Commissioners by George Gouldsmith Presbury Esquire who is appointed for that Purpose and that the said Platt and certificate thereof be entered on Record among the records of the said Town agreeably to the act of Assembly passed at November Session 1794 ch. 62, entitled a Supplement to the act entitled an act to empower the Commissioners of Baltimore Town &c &c——

Application by proprietors filed No. 95

21st. APRIL 1795.

The Commissioners Met   Present

WM SMITH   PHILIP GRAYBELL ⎱ Comrs —
THOMAS ELLIOT   DAVID MCMECHEN ⎰

The Commissioners of Baltimore Town being called on by Captain John Snider to fix the Corner of Market and Fell's Streets at their intersection on the South Side of Fells Street having taking the Depositions of Mr. Isaac Grist William Jacobs and Jonathan Harrison Do fix and determine a Stone Marked C R Standing at the Corner of Jonathan Harrisons house to be the Corner of the Intersection aforesaid— Adjourned to Thursday at 10 oClock ————

The depositions of Messrs. Grist Jacobs and Harrison are filed among the Commissioners Papers Nos. 92 & 3— ———

23rd APRIL 1795.

The Commissioners met   Present

WM. SMITH   PHILIP GRAYBELL ⎱ Comrs —
THOMAS ELLIOT   DAVID MCMECHEN ⎰

The Commissioners having met to Consider the present Situation of the Markets of the Town— Resolved to raise the rents of the stalls of the Center Market to the Sum of Sixteen Dollars Each pr. Annum— One half of the rent to be paid in hand and the remainder at the End of Six Months after the renting the same. Ordered that the rent of the Point Market be raised to the Sum of Ten dollars Each pr. Annum—

Five Dollars in advance and the remainder in Six Months thereafter— The Commissioners of Baltimore Town being applied to by the Proprietors of the Lotts on the Alley commonly called Public Alley Extending South from Baltimore Street to the Bason heretofore conveyed by John Mercer by Deed for the use of the Public to Condemn the Same as a High way for the use of the Town forever Resolved that the said Alley be and is hereby Condemned as a Public high way for the use of the said Town for Ever hereafter Resolved that the   be given to the Auctioneers of Baltimore Town that if they do not comply with the requisites of the act of Assembly by giving Bond with approved Security and filing their respective Oaths of office by the Seventh of May Next that Information will be given the attorney General to prosecute them for their Neglect of duty — — ———— ———

Application filed No 96

The Commissioners agree to allow Richard Moale Twenty Guineas per Annum for the years 1786. 1787. and 1788 for his Services as Clerk to the Commissioners and Ten Guineas pr. Annum since— The said Richard Moale is directed to state and produce his accounts against Next Meeting in Order to Settle the same and receive an Order for the Balance— An Order Given On James Long in favor of David Harris Esqr. for £5.12.6 for 15 days attendance as a Commissioner—

2nd. MAY 1795.

The Commissioners met

Present WM SMITH   WM GOODWIN   } Comrs —
         THOS. ELLIOT DAVID McMECHEN   }

The Commissioners having taken into Consideration the petition of the Butchers concerning the Rent and Manner of Payment of the rent: Resolved that as a Convenience of payment of said Rent that one fourth thereof be paid in advance, One fourth in three Months, One other fourth in Six Months and the remainder in Nine Months: That Each Butcher when he applies for a Stall or Shamble shall make Such application to the Clerks of the Markets for the Same specifying the Number of the Shamble, the rent, Terms of Payment and when taken, and shall Subscribe his Name to the Same; and that the said Clerks of the Markets return a copy of it to the Secretary of the Commissioners that upon Default of payment of the rent in Six Months after it is due the said Contract shall be Void and the said Clerk of the Market is hereby directed to re-enter and rent the same for the remainder of the Term: And at the End of Each Year the Several Clerks of the Markets return to the Secretary of the Commissioners a list of the Names of Such Persons who do not pay agreeably to their Contract and the Secretary is hereby directed to publish the same in One of the News Papers of the Town— Mr. George Mathews being appointed Inspector of Salted Provisions for Baltimore Town by the Governor and Council Produced the following Certificate: To wit I do hereby certify that George Mathews lately appointed Inspector of Salted Provisions for the Town of Baltimore did Solemnly and Truly affirm to the duties of his said office agreeable to Law. Given under my hand this first day of April 1795

Signed   GEO SALMON

Certificate filed No 100

4 JUNE 1795

The Commissioners Met

SAMUEL CHASE   WM GOODWIN   } Comrs —
Present THOMAS ELLIOT   DAVID MCMECHEN

The Board being informed that David Moore appointed by this board Inspector of flour and Thomas Buckingham his deputy, and George Mathews appointed by the Governor and Council inspector of Salted Provisions and John Morgan his deputy have neglected to take the Oath of Fidelity to this State as required by the 55 Article of the Constitution and form of Goverment and also by the act of Assembly of November 1781. cha: 12 Sec: 22 and by the act of Assembly of November 1786. cha: 17 Sec: 18. Ordered that the said David Moore, and Thomas Buckingham and George Mathews and John Morgan do appear before this Board on Saturday Morning next between the Hours of Ten and Eleven oClock at the Court house to inform the Board whether they have respectively taken the said Oath of Fidelity and if they have not of the Cause of their Neglect, and that the Secretary deliver a Copy of this Order to Each of the said Persons————

6th. June 1795.

The Commissioners met   Present

SAMUEL CHASE WM SMITH   PHILIP GRAYBELL }
WM GOODWIN THOS ELLIOT DAVID McMECHEN } Comrs —

David Moore appeared before the Board agreeably to the order of the last Meeting and informed the Board that he had not taken the Oath of fidelity mentioned in the 55 article of the Constitution and form of Goverment since his last appointment or for some years last past. The Board are unanimously of opinion that the said David Moor ought to have taken the Oath of fidelity mentioned in the constitution and form of Goverment before He acted as inspector of flour— The Board are unanimously of opinion that the said David Moore ought to have taken the Oath of fidelity mentioned in the 55 article of the Constitution and form of Goverment in Pursuance of the directions in the act of November Session 1781 cha : 12 Section 22. before He acted as inspector of Flour — — George Mathews appeared before the Board agreeably to the order of the Last Meeting and informed the Board that he had not taken the Oath of Fidelity mentioned in the 55 article of the Constitution and form of Goverment— The Board are unanimously of opinion that the Said George Mathews ought to have taken the Oath of Fidelity mentioned in the 55 article of the Constitution and form of Goverment before he acted as Inspector of Salted Provisions— The Board are of opinion that the said George Mathews ought to have taken the Oath of fidelity mentioned in the 55 article of the Constitution and form of Goverment in pursuance of the directions of the act of Assembly November Session 1786. Cha: 17. sec 18. before he acted as Inspector of Salted Provisions—

The Board then adjourned untill Monday Morning at 11 oClock A M— In consequence of the above Opinion of the Commissioners of Baltimore Town Mr. David Moor produced the following Certificate which was Ordered to be filed Viz "I hereby certify that David Moor Inspector of flour for Baltimore Town appeared before me and took the Oath of fidelity to the State of Maryland agreeably to the Constitution and form of Goverment and the act of Assembly of November Session 1781 ch. 12 directing the Same and also Subscribed his Belief in the Christian religion

Balto. June 8th. 1795   L S   GEORGE: SALMON—

JUNE 8th. 1795

The Commissioners Met

<table>
<tr><td rowspan="3">Present</td><td>SAML. CHASE</td><td>WM SMITH</td></tr>
<tr><td>PHILIP GRAYBELL</td><td>THOMAS ELLIOT</td></tr>
<tr><td>WM. GOODWIN</td><td>DAVID McMECHEN</td></tr>
</table>

The Board of Commissioners appoint Samuel Chase and William Goodwin Esquires to examine the Copy of the Proceedings of the Town Commissioners from the first of December 1729 to the Present Time with the Original Books and Papers and report to the Board whether the copy be Truly and faithfully made in the record Book by the Secretary of this Board

Ordered that the Secretary be allowed the Sum of Sixty Dollars for his Trouble making the copy of the above Proceedings of the Town Commissioners   The Commissioners agree to allow their Secretary in full Compensation for his Trouble at the rate of Thirty five Pounds per year to Commence from the 28th day of April last.

JULY 14th. 1795

The Commissioners of Baltimore Town met at the House of John Starke in Said Town

<table>
<tr><td rowspan="2">Present</td><td>THOMAS ELLIOT</td><td>PHILIP GRAYBELL</td><td rowspan="2">} Comrs.</td></tr>
<tr><td>WM. GOODWIN</td><td>DAVID McMECHEN</td></tr>
</table>

The Commissioners having first qualified according to the act of Assembly passed November Session 1781. Ch 12 for the Purpose of appointing a flour Inspector for the year ensuing for the Town of Baltimore appointed Mr. David Moore Inspector of flour and directed him to qualify as such and to return Such qualification immediately which is now done. Viz. I hereby certify that David Moore (inspector of flour for Baltimore County) has this day taken the Oaths as prescribed by law— Given under my hand this 14th. day of July 1795.

L. S.   GEO: SALMON—

OCTOBER 12th. 1795

The commissioners Met   Present

| Wm. Smith | Wm. Goodwin | } *Comrs* — |
| Thomas Elliot | Philip Graybell | |

Mr. Abraham Van Bibber and Others having petitioned the Commissioners of the Town to condemn Charles Street south from Pratt street to the utmost Limits of the Town and also an Alley called Liverpool Alley Extending South West Parallel with Charles street to an Alley called Peace Alley and also the said Alley called Peace Alley— Ordered that the said Petitioners have the Property thro which the said Street and Alleys are to pass surv·yed and laid off into Streets Lanes and Alleys as is directed ·y the acts of Assembly requiring the same and return a Pl: !t thereof to the Secretary of the Commissioners and that the secretary On return thereof give Notice in the News Papers that the Commissioners of Baltimore Town will meet on Monday the   day of   in Order to declare the same to be part of Baltimore Town— The Commissioners appoint James Norris weigher of hay for Baltimore Town and direct him to qualify as Such and to return such qualification to their Secretary Immediately which is now done as follows— I James Norris of Baltimore Town in Baltimore County and State of Maryland do solemnly Swear that I when required will well and truly according to the Best of my skill and Knowledge Weigh all hay which shall come to Hillen's Machine in the Town aforesaid without any fear, favor, affection Malice or Partiality whatever to the Buyer or Seller and that I will not willingly or wittingly charge, ask, take, receive exact or Demand any Other or larger fees or Rates for doing my duty than is Mentioned or directed by an Act of Assembly passed November Session 1771. Entitled an Act to prevent the Exportation of flour Staves or Shingles not Merchantable from the Town of Baltimore in Baltimore County and to regulate the weight of hay and Measure of Grain, salt, flaxseed and firewood within the said Town and to prevent the Exportation of flour not Merchantable from Fells Point in the said County— Sworn before me the subscriber this Eleventh day of November 1795.

           L S.   Geo: Gouldth: Presbury

BALTIMORE NOVEMBER 1st. 1795

The Commissioners met

SAMUEL CHASE	PHILIP GRAYBELL	} Comrs —
Present WM. GOODWIN	THOMAS ELLIOT	

The Commissioners being called on by Doctor Mathews to fix and Establish the South East Corner of Lexington and Liberty Streets at their Intersection having Measured the Streets adjoining fixed the Corner of the said Intersection by putting down a Stone Marked W. P. M. 1795 which they determine and Establish as the Corner aforesaid at the Intersection aforesaid— —

SAML VINCENT *Clk C. C.*

NOVEMBER 19th. 1795

The Commissioners met

SAMUEL CHASE	PHILIP GRAYBELL	} Comrs —
WM SMITH	THOMAS ELLIOT	

The Commissioners appoint John Gottro, Charles Merriken Godfry Hartung and Peter Weary Wood-Corders for Baltimore Town for the year Ensuing and direct them to qualify agreeably to the Act of Assembly Nov. Session 1771. cha: XX and return a Certificate of such qualification to the Secratary of this Board The Commissioners also appoint James Norris to be Weigher of Hay for the Town of Baltimore for the Ensuing Year agreeably to the act of Assembly directing the Same and direct him to Qualify accordingly and to return a Certificate of Such Qualification to the Secretary of this Board

BALTIMORE 23rd NOVEMBER 1795

The Commissioners Met

Present SAMUEL CHASE	WILLIAM GOODWIN	} Comrs —
WILLIAM SMITH	PHILIP GRAYBELL	

The Commissioners appoint Richard Bouldin a Weigher of hay for the Town of Baltimore for the year Ensuing and direct him to qualify according to the act of Assembly directing the Same, and to return such Qualification to their Secretary immediately— —

The Commissioners appoint William Wright Clerk of the Point Market for the Year Ensuing and direct him to give

Bond with approved Security and to qualify according to act of Assembly requiring the Same and to return such Qualifications to their Secretary Immediately— The Commissioners allow the said Clerk the Sum of Twenty Pounds per Annum for his Services— Bond filed with Commissioners Papers No. 113

Richard Bouldins Oath of Office as a Weigher of hay filed with the Commissioners Papers No. 112 Wrights Oath of office No. 113 The several Oaths of office of Charles Merriken John Gottro and Peter Weary Wood Corders for Baltimore Town for the Year Ensuing are filed with the Commissioners Papers Numbers 114—115—116— — —— — ——

28th NOVEMBER 1795

The Commissioners Met   Present

WILLIAM SMITH   SAMUEL CHASE   } Comrs —
PHILIP GRAYBELL   WILLIAM GOODWIN }

The Commissioners of Baltimore Town having considered the Petition of the Proprietors of the Lott Number fifty Six praying a Condemnation of an Alley called Exchange Alley of the width of Twelve feet runing thro Part of the said Lott Number fifty Six to Commence from the End of fifty Eight feet from the North East Corner of the whole Lott on a Lane which was formerly called Sharping Lane but now Second Street and runing thence Westerly bounding on said Street Twelve feet, thence runing Southerly two hundred and fifty One feet or thereabouts to Water Street, thence runing and bounding On Water Street twelve feet and thence with a Straight Line to the Begining Do hereby Condemn the said Alley of the width aforesaid and runing as aforesaid as a Public Highway for the use of Baltimore Town forever hereafter— Petition filed No 118—Platt filed.

I hereby certify to whom it may concern that I have deputed George Washington Moor Inspector of Flour for the Port of Baltimore

Signed   DAVID MOOR

Baltimore November 17th. 1795.

Baltimore County

I do hereby certify that the within mentioned George Washington Moor appeared before me the Subscriber One of the Justices of the County aforesaid and took the oath of office as deputy Inspector of flour for Baltimore Town and the Oaths to Government and Subscribed his belief in the Christian Religeon.

Signed

JOHN MOALE

November 17th. 1796.   Certificate filed with Commissioners Papers—

BALTIMORE TOWN MARCH 11th. 1796.

The Commissioners met

Present WILLIAM SMITH   WILLIAM GOODWIN ⎱ *Esqrs.*
        PHILIP GRAYBELL DAVID McMECHEN ⎰

The Commissioners having met to appoint an Inspector of Salted Provisions, unanimously appointed Mr. George Mathews Inspector of Salted Provisions for Baltimore Town for the Year ensuing and direct him to Qualify accordingly, and return such Qualification to their Secretary— The inspector of Salted Provisions is directed to settle his accounts with the Secretary of the Commissioners and to pay him the Amount— The Secretary is directed to pay Mr. William McCreery the Amount of his account out of the Monies arrising from the Point Market I hereby Certify that George Mathews Inspector of Salted Provisions of Baltimore Town hath affirmed to the duties of his office according to the several acts of Assembly; hath affirmed to Support the Constitution of the united states and declared his belief in the Christian Religeon before me the 24th. day of March 1796

Signed

GEO: SALMON

——— " ———

BALTIMORE 6th. JUNE 1796—

The Commissioners met

Present WILLIAM SMITH   DAVID McMECHEN ⎱ *Esqrs.*
        PHILIP GRAYBELL WILLIAM GOODWIN ⎰

The Commissioners of Baltimore Town being called on by Mr. Robert Mickle to Establish the North East Corner of Baltimore Street and Charles street at their Intersection, having Measured the width of Baltimore Street from the Brick Store

built by John Ridgely and also the Width of Charles Street
from the Brick Store Owned by Daniel Deady fixed the said
Corner at the distance of Sixty Six feet North from the said
John Ridgely's Brick Store, and forty Nine feet Six Inches
West from the said Daniel Deady's Store on Baltimore Street
which they now fix as the Corner of Baltimore and Charles
Streets at the Intersection aforesaid—— ——

BALTIMORE JULY 11th. 1796—

At a Meeting of the Commissioners of Baltimore Town
    Present

WILLIAM SMITH PHILIP GRAYBELL
THOMAS ELLIOT DAVID McMECHEN

The Commissioners having met to appoint an Inspector of
flour for the Town of Baltimore for the year ensuing, David
Moor was unanimously appointed Inspector of Flour for the
Town and Port of Baltimore and is directed to Qualify
according, and to return such Qualifications to the secretary
of the Commissioners— David Moor immediately qualified as
Inspector of flour as directed before Thomas Elliot Esq. One
of the Commissioners—

BALTIMORE 3rd. OCTOBER 1796—

The Commissioners met

       WILLIAM SMITH   PHILIP GRAYBELL } *Esqrs.*
Present THOMAS ELLIOT   DAVID McMECHEN }

The Commissioners having taken into Consideration the propriety of changing the Name of Lancaster Alley and Shakespear Alley into Lancaster Street and Shakespear Street agreeably to the Prayer of the Petition of the Proprietors of the
Lotts on the Same resolve that the said Names be changed and
that in future the said Alleys be called and Known only by
the Names of Lancaster Street and Shakespear for Ever hereafter—Petition filed with Commissioners Papers — — — — —

BALTIMORE 31st. OF OCTOBER 1796.

The Commissioners Met

       WILLIAM SMITH   DAVID McMECHEN
Present THOMAS ELLIOTT   PHILIP GRAYBELL

The Commissioners of Baltimore being called on by James
Hicks to fix and Establish high and Low Streets at their North

and West Intersection and having Measured the streets and Lotts adjoining find the North and West Corner of the house standing on the Corner of Lott No. 62 owned by Frederick Hansbaugh and occupied by James Renshaw is the Intersection of the said Streets and do now fix and Establish the said North and West Corner of the said house as the Corner of Said Streets at their intersection aforesaid — — — — —— ———

BALTIMORE 10th. NOVEMBER 1796.

The Commissioners met

WM. GOODWIN   SAMUEL CHASE   ⎱
Present PHILIP GRAYBELL   THOMAS ELLIOTT   ⎰ *Comm srs*

The Commissioners appoint John Gottro Charles Merriken Godfry Hartung and Peter Weary Wood-Corders for Baltimore Town for the year ensuing and direct them to qualify accordingly and return their Qualification to the Secretary immediately— They also appoint Richard Bouldin weigher of hay for Baltimore Town for the year ensuing and direct him to qualify accordingly and return his qualification to the Secretary of Baltimore Town. they also appoint James Long and William Wright Clerks of the Markets for Baltimore Town and direct them to qualify accordingly and return their Qualification to the Secretary of the Com m srs of Baltimore Town

Baltimore County to wit   November 23rd 1796.

Personally appeared before me the Subscriber One of the Justices of the peace for the County aforesaid Peter Weary one of the Wood Corders for Baltimore Town and made oath on the Holy Evangels of Almighty God that he will when required in a Just and an Impartial Manner well and truly Set up, pack Cord and Measure all fire Wood brought for sale to Baltimore Town, according to the best of his skill and Knowledge and the directions of the act of Assembly of 1771. Ch: 20, and that he will not ask, receive take exact or demand any other or larger fees or rates for doing his duty in his said office of Wood Corder than is directed by the said act.

(Signed)   JAS CALHOUN

Baltimore County to wit   November 14th. 1796.

Personally appeared before me the Subscriber one of the Justices of the peace for Baltimore County Charles Merriken one of the Wood Corders for Baltimore Town and made Oath on the Holy Evangel of Almighty God that he will when required in a Just and an Impartial manner well and truly set up, pack, Cord and Measure all firewood brought for sale to the town of Baltimore according to the best of his skill and knowledge and the directions of the act of Assembly passed November Session 1771 ch: 20. and that he will not willingly or wittingly Charge, ask demand take, Exact or receive any Other or larger fees or rates for doing his duty in his said office of Wood-Corder than is directed by the said act

(Signed)   CHARLES MERRIKEN

Sworn and Subscribed before

(Signed)   GEO. GOULD PRESBURY

Charles Merriken also took the Several Oaths to goverment appointed to be taken, before me and Subscribed and repeated his belief in the Christian Religeon

(Signed)   GEO. G. PRESBURY

At a Meeting of the Commissioners of Baltimore Town on Friday the 13th. of January 1797.

Present   SAMUEL CHASE   DANIEL BOWLEY   }
THOMAS ELLIOTT   DAVID MCMECHEN   *Comrs* —
WM. GOODWIN

In Virtue of an Act of Assembly entitled "an act to Erect Baltimore Town in Baltimore County into a City and to incorporate the Inhabitants thereof" and of the division of the said City into Eight Wards by special Commissioners appointed by the Governor and Council and returned to the Commissioners of Baltimore Town, they proceeded to appoint three Judges in Each of the said Wards to hold an Election for the choice of the Members of the first branch of the City Council and also for the choice of Electors of the Mayor of the City and of the Members of the second branch of the City Council agreeably to the said act of Assembly as follows to wit—

ELIAS ELLICOTT ⎫
JOHN P. PLEASANTS ⎬ Judges in the first Ward
GEO DECKER ⎭

LYDE GOODWIN ⎫
SAMUEL OWINGS ⎬ Judges in the Second ward
CHRISTIAN KEENER ⎭

ZEB: HOLLINGSWORTH ⎫
JOHN SWANN ⎬ Judges in the Third ward
JOHN MERRYMAN ⎭

GEO. SALMON ⎫
HENRY NICOLS ⎬ Judges in the fourth ward
SAMUEL HOLLINGSWORTH ⎭

THOROUGHGOOD SMITH ⎫
ARCHIBALD CAMPBELL ⎬ Judges in the fifth ward
GERRARD HOPKINS ⎭

GEO. G. PRESBURY ⎫
RICHARD CARSON JUNR. ⎬ Judges in the sixth ward
ENGLEHARD YEISER ⎭

RICHARD CATON ⎫
CHRISTIAN MYERS ⎬ Judges in the Seventh ward
DAVID BROWN ⎭

JOB SMITH ⎫
JOSEPH BYASS ⎬ Judges in the Eighth ward
HEZEKIAH WATERS ⎭

The Commissioners of Baltimore Town having met on the East side of Jones's Falls on Saturday the 14th. of January 1797——

Present WM. SMITH   DAVID MCMECHEN ⎫ Comrs —
         PHILIP GRAYBELL WM. GOODWIN ⎭

The Commissioners of Baltimore Town being called on by Charles Jessop to fix and Establish the North East Corner of Bridge and high Streets at their intersection, and having first Measured the streets adjoining planted a Stone upon Part of an Iron Crow Bar drove into the Earth, which Crow Bar and Stone they now fix and Establish as the Corner of the said Streets at the Intersection aforesaid——

The Commissioners met at the house of their Secretary on Monday the 23rd. day of January 1797.

         WILLIAM SMITH   PHILIP GRAYBELL ⎫ Comrs —
Present WM. GOODWIN   DAVID MCMECHEN ⎭

The Commissioners unanimously appoint Eliu Underwood Weigher of hay for Baltimore Town for the year Ensuing and direct him to qualify Accordingly and to file such qualification with their Secretary immediately.

Baltimore County to wit

          On this 24th day of January 1797 Personally appeared before me the Subscriber One of the Justices of the Peace for Baltimore County aforesaid Eliu Underwood One of the Hay Weighers for Baltimore Town aforesaid and Solemnly affirmed and declared that he when required will well and Truly according to the best of his skill and Knowledge

Weigh all hay brought to Baltimore Town for Sale, without any fear, favor affection Malice or Partiality whatever to the Buyer or Seller and that he will not Willingly or Wittingly, charge, ask, demand take receive or Exact any Other or larger fees or rates for doing his duty in his said office as weigher of hay than is Mentioned and directed by the act of Assembly of November Session 1771 chap 20—

[Signed]   GEO. G: PRESBURY

Eliu Underwood took the Several Affirmations appointed to be taken to Goverment before me this 24th. day of January 1797 and declared his belief in the Christian Religion

Signed   GEO G. PRESBURY

The Powers heretofore Vested in the Commissioners of Baltimore Town Except as to holding the Election for Delegates to the General Assembly of Maryland having ceased and determined by the operation of the Corporation, of the City of Baltimore Their Secretary was directed to deliver their Records, Papers proceedings and Vouchers to Richard H. Moale the Person appointed by an Ordinance of the said Corporation to receive the Same, which is now accordingly done

City of Baltimore   R. H. MOALE Secretary.

March 20th. 1797   To the Commissioners of Balt Town

17th SEPTEMBER 1798

The Commissioners Met   Present

WILLIAM GOODWIN   DAVID McMECHEN

DAVID WILLIAMSON   THOMAS USHER

Captain Philip Graybell having resigned the Commissioners proceeded to the Choice of a Commissioner in his place, when Captain Thomas Cole was unanimously Elected and qualified as such before Geo. G. Presbury Esqr accordingly

At a Meeting of the Commissioners of Baltimore Town On Saturday the 11th. day of November 1797 within the City of Baltimore were present

SAML. CHASE   WILLIAM GOODWIN ⎫ Comrs —
PHILIP GRAYBELL   DAVID McMECHEN ⎰

The said Commissioners having first taken the Oath to Elect two Commissioners in the places of Daniel Bowley and William Smith Esqrs. who had resigned, they made Choice of Richard Caton and Thomas Usher as Commissioners for Baltimore who qualified as such accordingly—

13th. NOVEMBER 1798

The Commissioners Met   Present

THOMAS ELLIOTT   DAVID MCMECHEN
RICHARD CATON   THOMAS USHER

Mr Samuel Chase having resigned The Commissioners met to make choice of a Commissioner in his place, when David Williamson was duly Elected who qualified as such before James Calhoun Esqr. accordingly——

INDEX.

Comparative Plat of the Original Sixty Acres 1729-1905.

This map gives approximately the outlines of Baltimore Town, and shows how the site appears in 1905. The dotted lines within the space indicate the narrow original streets, and the direction in which each was widened. The point of the beginning of the survey of Baltimore Town—shown on the plat—has been established by a Commission and a stone (suitably inscribed) planted, as will appear on the Land Records of Baltimore city. The point is about 165 feet from the north side of Pratt street, and about 70 feet east from the east side of Charles street.

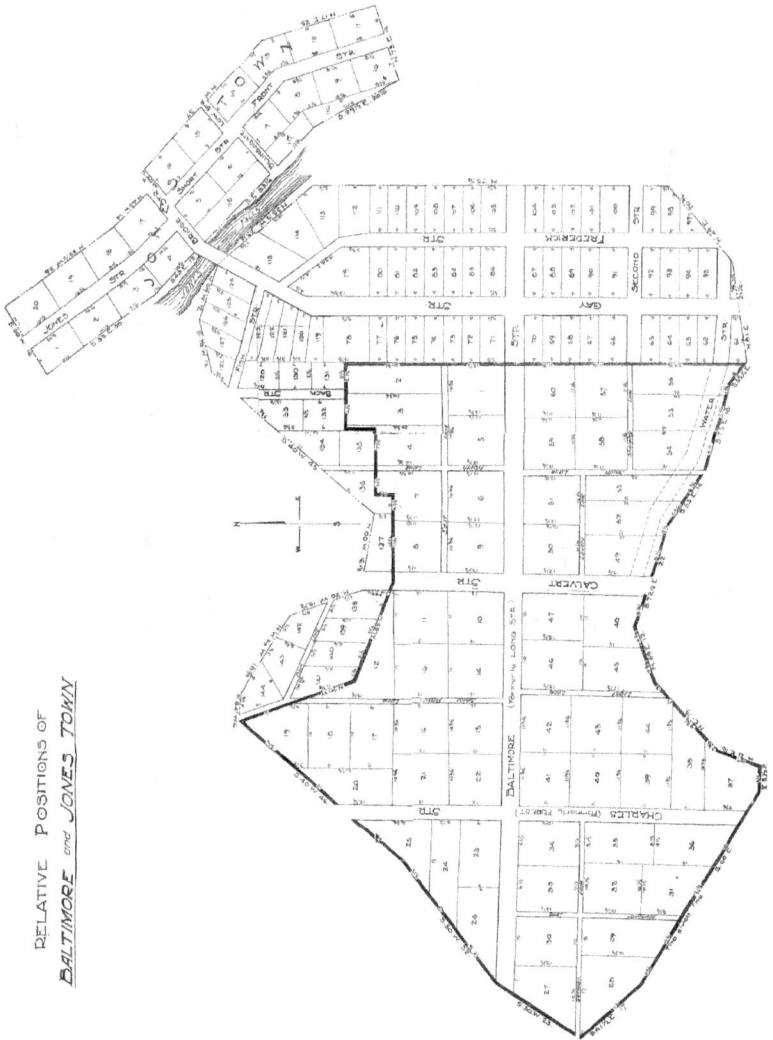

RELATIVE POSITIONS OF
BALTIMORE and *JONES TOWN*

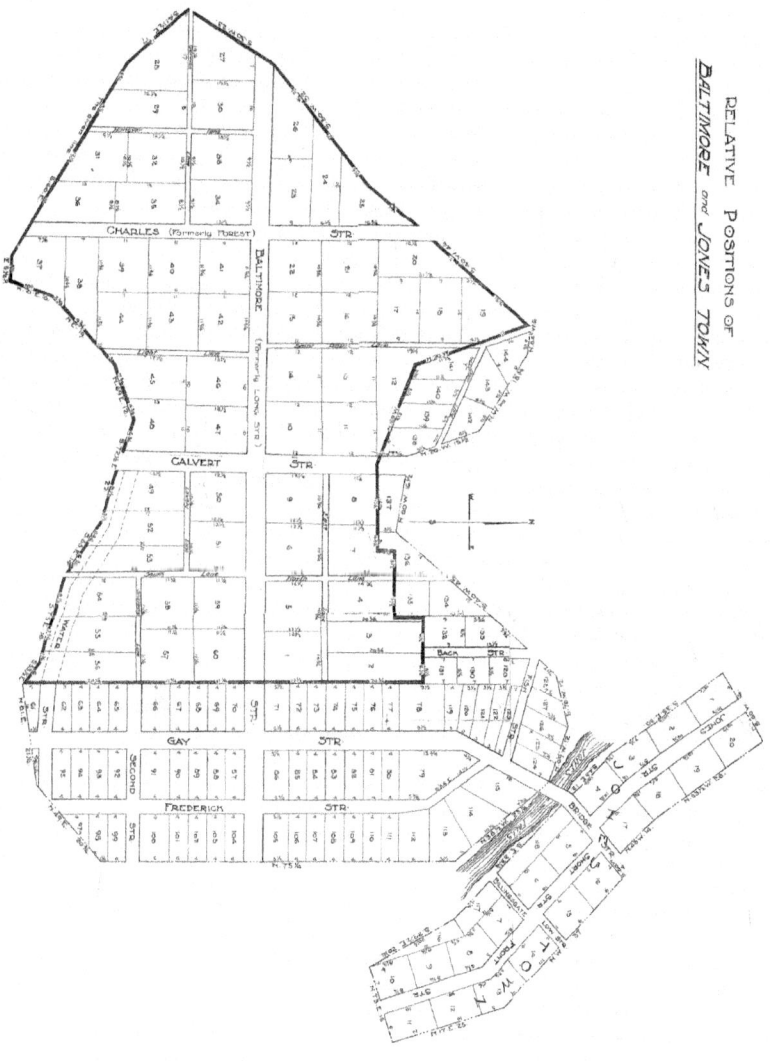

RELATIVE POSITIONS OF
BALTIMORE and JONES TOWN

CHARLES (Formerly Forest) STR · BALTIMORE (Formerly Long Str) · CALVERT STR · GAY STR · FREDERICK STR

showing relative positions of Baltimore and Jones Town as first laid out, with additions between the two as surveyed by Ruxton Gay, after the consolidation. (Original Jones Town did not include lots 1, 6, 117, 118 above the Falls. The heavy line indicates original site of Baltimore.

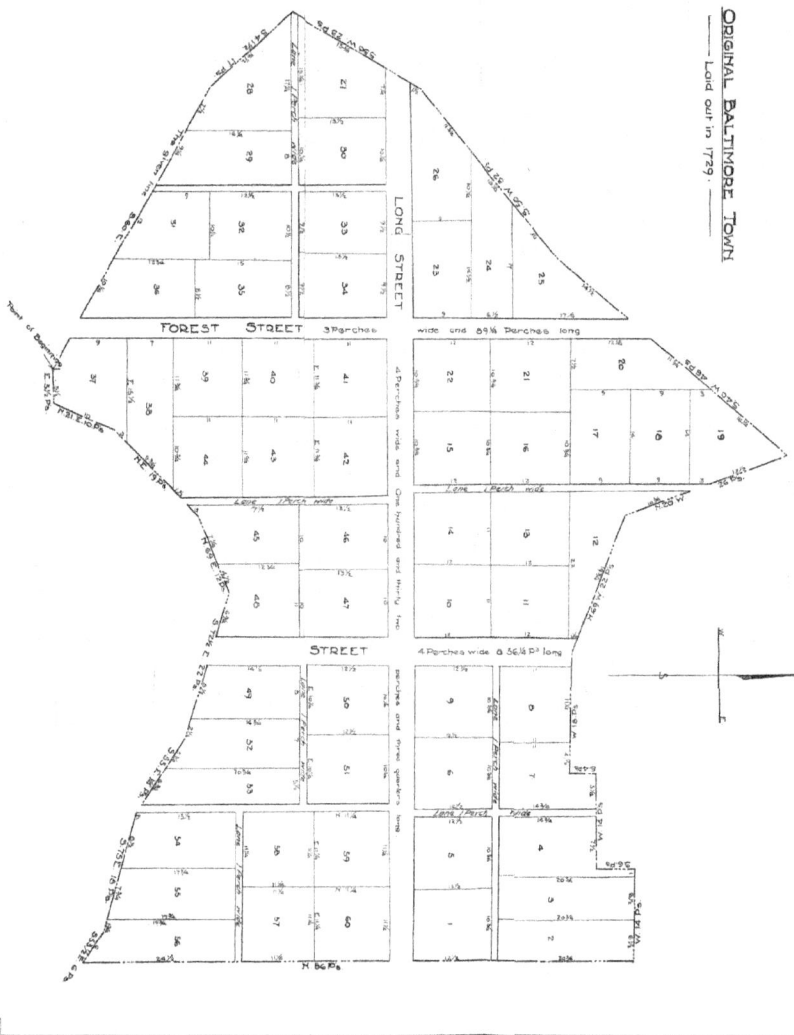

ORIGINAL BALTIMORE TOWN
— Laid out in 1729. —

Original Baltimore Town, showing lots as laid out in 1729.

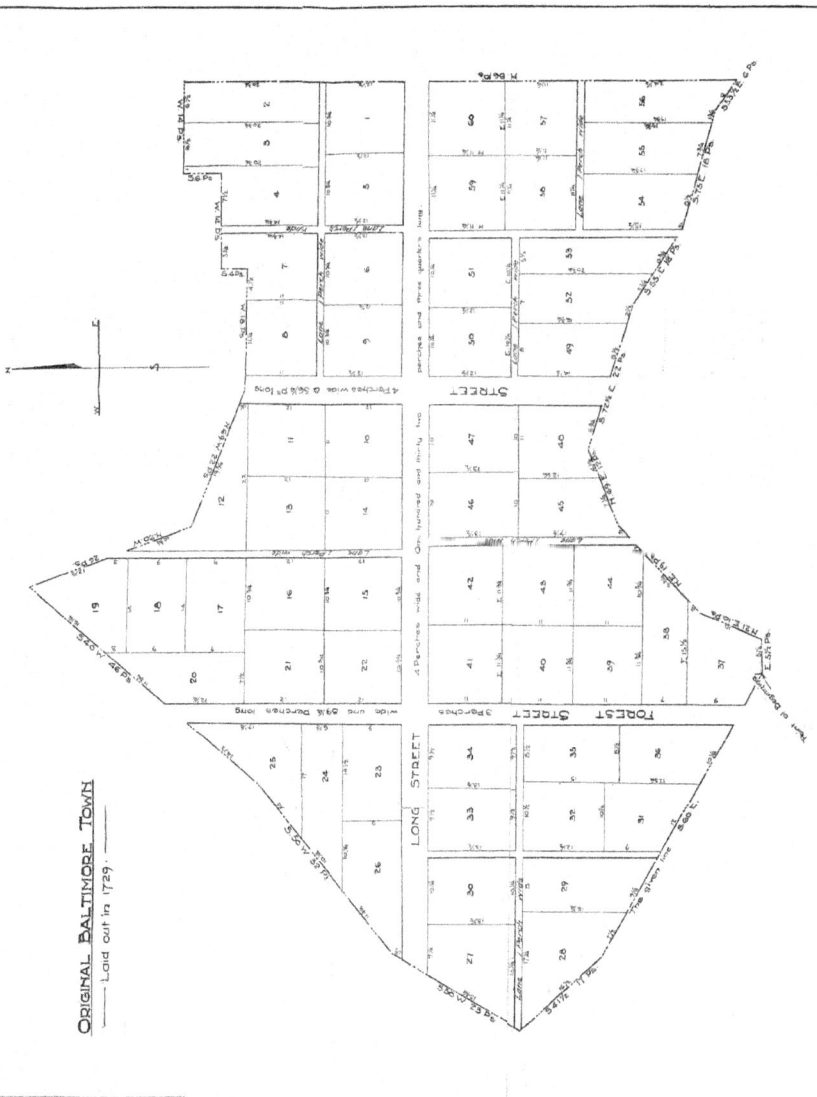

ORIGINAL BALTIMORE TOWN
——— Laid out in 1729. ———

www.ingramcontent.com/pod-product-compliance
Lightning Source LLC
Chambersburg PA
CBHW072123090426
42739CB00012B/3052